SEXUAL DETOX

A Guide for Guys Who Are Sick of Porn

Tim Challies
Cruciform Press | Released October, 2010

This book is dedicated to my son's generation,
a generation of boys who will avoid the allure of
pornography only by the grace of God.
– Tim Challies

D1260964

CruciformPress

"In an age when sex is worshiped as a god, a little book like this can go a long way to helping men overcome sexual addiction."
   Pastor Mark Driscoll, Mars Hill Church

"Tim Challies strikes just the right balance in this brief but necessary work. His assessment of the sexual epidemic in our culture is sober but not without hope. His advice is practical but avoids a checklist mentality. His discussion of sexual sin is frank without being inappropriate. In a day when it can almost be assumed that every young male struggles with pornography, lust, and masturbation, this book will be a valuable resource. I'm grateful for Tim's wisdom, candor, and grace."
   Kevin DeYoung, Senior Pastor, University Reformed Church, East Lansing, Michigan; Conference Speaker and author of numerous books, including *The Good News We Almost Forgot, Just Do Something*, and *Why We Love the Church*

"In an era in which every man is online, pornography is not just a problem for Christian men; it is THE problem. All men face the temptation of this mind polluting, heart-hardening, soul-deadening sin. Many men, young and old, in our churches need *Sexual Detox*. This is a welcomed book. In a short, compressed format Challies identifies the toxic nature of this sin and offers practical, doable and, above all, gospel-centered hope for men. I want every man I serve and all the guys on our staff to read this book."
   Tedd Tripp, Pastor, Grace Fellowship Church, Hazle Township, Pennsylvania; Conference Speaker and author of *Shepherding a Child's Heart* and *Instructing a Child's Heart*

"Thank God for using Tim to articulate simply and unashamedly the truth about sex amidst a culture of permissiveness. This book is simple and biblical in its approach to "detox" us of the lies we hold onto in this area of sexuality. Read it and believe it."
   Ben Zobrist, All-Star Right Fielder, Tampa Bay Rays

"The church, the bride of Christ, finds itself in a sexual age. Much as we Christians might struggle to accept this, sex is very nearly the dominant cultural currency of our day. Because we know that this is a perversion of God's good plan, we might struggle to accept this reality—and to confront it as we must. *Sexual Detox* is just what we need. It is clear, honest, and biblical, written with a tone that is knowing but kind, exhortative but gracious, realistic but determined. Those of us who work with youth—the target market in the sex-saturated society—have been given by Tim Challies a terrific resource for fighting sin and exalting Christ. We are in Tim's debt. Here's hoping that this book and its emphasis on confrontational holiness will spread far and wide for the health of the church and the strengthening of marriages both temporal and divine."

> **Owen Strachan,** Instructor of Christian Theology and Church History, Boyce College; Co-author of the *Essential Edwards Collection*

"Tim has worked hard to express these truths simply. You can thank us for that. He has seen from teaching us that we are simple guys who need a simple explanation of God's desires for our sexuality. We are convinced that if you are a normal guy with normal guy problems and a normal guy worldview, this book will be helpful for you, as it has been for us."

> **John Cowle, Steve Funston, Nick Mitchell,** and **Julian Freeman** Twenty-something guys from the church in Toronto where Tim Challies is an elder (From the Foreword).

Cruciform**Press**
something new in Christian publishing

Our Books: Short. Clear. Concise. Helpful. Inspiring. Gospel-focused. *Print, ebook, audiobook.*

Monthly Releases: A new book the first day of every month.

Consistent Prices: Every book costs the same.

Subscription Options: Print books or ebooks delivered to you every month, at a discount. Or buy one at a time.

Annual or Monthly Subscriptions
Print Book . . . . $6.49 per month
Ebook . . . . $3.99 per month

Non-Subscription Sales
1-5 Print Books . . . . $8.45 each
6-50 Print Books . . . . $7.45 each
More than 50 Print Books . . . . $6.45 each

Sexual Detox: A Guide for Guys Who Are Sick of Porn

Print ISBN:	978-1-453807-28-6
ePub ISBN:	978-1-936760-01-5
Mobipocket ISBN:	978-1-936760-00-8

Published by Cruciform Press, Adelphi, Maryland. Copyright © 2010 by Tim Challies. All rights reserved. Unless otherwise indicated, all Scripture quotations are taken from: *The Holy Bible: English Standard Version*, Copyright © 2001 by Crossway Bibles, a division of Good News Publishers. Used by permission. All rights reserved. Italics or bold text within Scripture quotations indicates emphasis added.

Table of Contents

FOREWORD

Why This Book?

Picture a group of 20-something-year-old guys sitting in a room brainstorming together on how to write a killer Foreword for an important book that has helped us replace worldly lies with biblical truth about sexuality. As we bat some ideas around, Steve brings out his famous half-cooked chocolate chip cookies and sets them before me, John, the token diabetic of the group. Immediately I am faced with a decision. Should I indulge and enjoy these chocolaty delights (the memories of which cause me to slip in and out of a mini flavour-coma) or should I resist and do what I know is the best thing for me?

This decision, like all decisions, is based on more than mere knowledge. It is based on belief. If I take a cookie, it means I believe that eating it is the best thing for me—or at the very least, that the pleasure it will give is greater than the consequences to my health.

In *Sexual Detox*, Tim Challies addresses men who know that sexual fantasies, masturbation, and pornography are wrong, but choose to indulge in their sin regardless. The purpose of this book is not to get you to admit sexual sin is wrong—you already know that. The purpose is to move you to *believe* biblical truth about sexuality and have these beliefs determine your decisions.

When you indulge in sexual sin, it reveals what you truly believe about sexuality. You believe that the pleasure of sin is better than the pleasure of obeying God by enjoying sex the way God created it to be enjoyed. You believe that the pleasure you derive from your sin is greater than the consequences your sin will have on you and those around you. You believe that your momentary pleasure is greater than the rewards the Lord has for you—both in this life and in the life to come.

We all know sexual sin is wrong but we need to understand *why* it is wrong and that God has created sexuality for something *greater*. To help us replace a worldly view of sex with a God-defined understanding of sexuality is the reason Tim wrote this book.

Why Tim?

Many of you will know Tim from his blog or from other books and articles he's written. You will already know that he is a gifted and compelling writer, able to present the truths of Scripture with clarity and conviction. What you won't know is what *we* have all seen through the years we have known him as a friend, mentor, and pastor. Tim is a man who works hard to study the truth, to apply it to his own life, and then to teach what he has learned and applied in order to help others. Because Tim believes these things, lives these things, and loves to bless other men in his life (like us) he is especially qualified to write this book.

Why You?

We are writing this Foreword to you to commend this book as highly as we can. Not primarily because it is some new cure-all, can't-miss, one-step solution to all your problems with sexual sin, but because it represents what Tim has taught us that has helped us: It is biblical truth. And that alone is what will change your heart, your desires, your beliefs.

Tim has worked hard to express these truths simply. You can thank us for that. He has seen from teaching us that we are simple guys who need a simple explanation of God's desires for our sexuality. We are convinced that if you are a normal guy with normal guy problems and a normal guy worldview, this book will be helpful for you, as it has been for us.

The bottom line is that when we believe in our hearts that the biblical view of sexuality is better than our sinful view of sex, we won't cease to be tempted, but we will stop *indulging* in sin. When we believe that the joy of obedience and the rewards of purity are greater, the draw of sexual sin will be lesser. When we believe all that God has planned for us and our sexuality we will, in Christ, become conquerors over temptation.

If that sounds like something you need, then we encourage you to take this book, to read it, and to have your mind and your heart detoxified, purified, and made ready for service to God who made you a sexual being—for his glory.

John Cowle, Steve Funston, Nick Mitchell, Julian Freeman

Members of Grace Fellowship Church
Toronto, Ontario

One
REALITY

I often thank God that I grew up in the years before the Internet was in every home; I'm not sure I would have handled it very well. It's not like I'm ancient, either, but my thirty-four years do mean that I was born and raised in a different world. It is difficult to quantify or even qualify how the world has changed since the web tied us all together into this strange and elaborate network of bits and bytes, but I do know that nearly every area of life has been touched by it. We do not have the old world plus the Internet; we have a whole new world. Even something as human as sex has been radically altered by this digital reality.

Teenagers in the 90s (when I was growing up) were not much different from teens today. We wanted the same things—we just had to work a little harder to get some of them. If we wanted to see pornography (and we did), the process usually involved at least two kids working in tandem. One would distract a shopkeeper while the other tried to steal a magazine from the rack at the back of the store. The appointed thief would have to pick up the magazine silently, shove it down his pants, and walk out of the store without being spotted. This was dangerous, high stakes work that, if anything went wrong, could easily result in a really awkward meeting between you, your parents, and the police.

Today, as you know, unless there are unhackable firewalls or sophisticated filters, a guy needs only to turn on his computer and, within two or three clicks of the mouse, he can have unlimited access to unlimited amounts of pornography. Porn merchants established a beachhead on the Internet in its earliest days, and have been aggressively building their billion-dollar digital empires ever since. As a result, it is actually far more difficult to avoid pornography than it is to find it, and it would be literally impossible for one person to watch all the pornography being created today; there would not be enough hours in the day or days in the year. Not even close. Needless to say, teens, and teenage boys in particular, are quick to sample this illicit feast.

Even pre-teen boys are being drawn in. From the first awakenings of sexuality, many pre-teens are inundated with pornography. These are not the images of coyly posed naked women that were common a couple of generations ago, but hard-core images that are often crude, base, and degrading. The sexuality of a whole generation of children is being formed not by talks with their parents, not by reading the kind of book I was given as a young man, but by professional pornographers who will do anything—anything!—to fuel an increased desire for increased depravity.

You don't need to be a conservative Christian to be deeply troubled by all this. A short time ago I read an article by a woman who considered herself a feminist. She insisted that she enjoyed sleeping with men and thought little of sleeping with a continual succession of men. Yet she shared what for her was a growing concern. More and more, she said, the men she slept with had no real interest in her at all. They simply wanted her to act like a porn star for their benefit. They were using her to do little more than act out their porn-fueled fantasies. There was no tenderness, no desire for shared intimacy, and certainly no love. They simply used her body as a means to a very immediate end. This, she saw, is quickly becoming the new norm. What seems clear is that a generation of men, drowning in a cesspool of porn, has begun forming a new set of expectations for what they want from women. They want women to subvert themselves in order to act like porn stars. The women walk away used, feeling like little more than prostitutes.

Indeed, because of porn, even prostitutes are finding their world changing. In the bestseller, *Super-Freakonomics*, Steven Levitt and Stephen Dubner devote most of a chapter to the economics of prostitution. One thing they have studied is the average price of specific sex acts charged by prostitutes over time. It seems that the taboo nature of certain acts has always claimed a premium. Yet "taboo" is a moving target. Acts that were once culturally forbidden because of their exceedingly vulgar and degrading nature are now accepted as legitimate forms of sexual expression. Therefore, what was once the most expensive act is now among the least expensive. In the world of prostitution, what would by any other standard be considered normal is now boring and undesirable. It has been replaced by the invasive, the degrading.

In the prices charged by prostitutes, Levitt and Dubner have found a way to measure the speed at which porn is warping the world's view of sexuality. How fast is that? Really fast. From taboo to mainstream in less than one lifetime. It makes you wonder what could change in your own lifetime.

Preparing for Detox

So, while it has never been easy being a guy, today the challenges to guys who want to be holy, who want to honor God with their minds and bodies, are tougher than ever. You live at a time and in a culture that is largely given over to sex. It's all around you, and you can hardly avoid its lure.

If you are like most young men, you have already started to give in to temptation. Perhaps you have only just begun to look at pornography, or perhaps you've been doing so for many years. Perhaps you struggle with masturbation. You don't really want to indulge yourself, but somehow it's a whole lot tougher to quit than you would have thought. Perhaps you are finding that, more than ever, sex is filling your mind and affecting your heart.

This book is intended primarily for young men, married or not, though I think there is benefit for men of any age. For you single guys, yes, we will talk a lot about marriage, but for three good reasons — most of you *will* get married, marriage is the central human institution, and sexuality and marriage are obviously inseparable. So, regardless of the status on your tax form, I want you to know that despite all the challenges posed by pornography, there is a better way, a way of escape. The means of grace God richly provides can equip you to face the reality and bear the burdens of living at this particular time in this fallen world. This short guide can help you discover (or rediscover) God's plan for sex and sexuality. I want to help you track down the lies you have believed about sex so those lies can be replaced by truth that comes straight from God, the one who created sex for us. I hope to help you reorient your understanding of sex, both in the big picture and in the act itself, according to God's plan for this great gift.

I suppose you noticed the word *Detox* in this book's title. Detoxification actually takes place in your body every day as various organs transform or get rid of things that aren't good for you. When someone has been chemically poisoned or exposed to too much radiation, the body needs some help, and detoxification becomes more intentional, more of a medical procedure. A third kind of detox is the popular meaning. This kind of detox takes place when someone is trying to be freed of addiction to drugs or alcohol. In each case, the basic idea is the same. Something has gotten inside you that doesn't belong there and needs to be removed. If it stays or builds up, you will only get sicker. You might even die.

Detox is therefore a reset to normal, a return to health. It's the reversal of a corrupting, polluting process. It gets you back to where you ought to be.

A huge percentage of men need a porn detox, a moral and psychological reset. In fact, I suspect that a large majority, even of Christian men, share this desperate need. Are you among them? If so, whether you recognize it or not, pornography has corrupted your thinking, weakened your conscience, warped your sense of right and wrong, and twisted your understanding and expectations of sexuality. You need a reset by the One who created sex.

In this book, I want to help you detox from all the junk you've seen, all the lies you've believed. This is not an easy process. It is rarely a quick process. It involves a letting go of old realities and an embrace of a new normal, the original normal. To be willing to go through it, you need to see how bad your current situation really is, and how the path you are on leads to no place good. You need to see that the path of porn leads only to more isolation, guilt, alienation, and pain. Whether you are single or married, such a reset to normal is the only thing that can equip you to ever become a pure, loving, attentive, sacrificial husband.

But then, you already know you need to change. Few Christian men indulge in pornography without realizing they need to quit. Every Christian guy who looks at porn wants to stop, but many of us want to stop just a little bit less than we want to keep going. The problem isn't knowledge—it's desire and ability. And so sin prevails.

Here's a promise. You will never stop until you begin to see the monstrous nature of the sin you are committing. You will never stop until the sin is more horrifying to you than the commission of the sin is enjoyable. You will need to hate that sin before you can find freedom from it. That means you need more grace. You need to cry out to be changed so you do see the monstrous nature of this sin, and then you need to *act*, in faith that God will meet you with grace as you seek to cut off the pornography and begin the reset.

The Monster in Disguise

The issue of pornography is spoken about so often in Christian circles that it is in danger of becoming cliché. But the actual human dangers— physical, emotional, psychological, and spiritual—are realities we must not avoid or overlook. We simply cannot allow pornography to become (or remain!) integrated into our lives. We must recognize it for the monstrosity it is. One helpful way to think about pornography is to see it as inherently *mocking*, *violent*, and *progressive*.

Mocking Pornography makes a mockery of God's intention for sex. Indeed, all the messages of pornography go directly against God's purposes. Here are just a couple of examples.

- Where God says the purpose of sex is to build unity between a husband and a wife, pornography says it is about fulfilling any perceived need with any partner, willing or unwilling. Indeed, pornography teaches that sex is everything except intimate body-to-body, soul-to-soul contact between willing spouses.

- God says sexual desire is good in a controlled context because it urges a man to pursue his wife (and a wife her husband). But pornography says sexual desire cannot and should not be controlled, but should be allowed to draw us to anyone we find attractive.

Violent Pornography reshapes our very understanding of sex, of manhood, and of womanhood. It is inherently violent, inherently unloving. It is not about mutual love and caring and commitment, but about conquests and vanquishing, about "having *your* way" (a revealing phrase) with someone else. It tears love from sex, leaving sex as the immediate gratification of base desires. It lives beyond rules and ethics and morality. It exists far beyond love. In this way, it is a perversion of sexuality, not a true form of it, and one that teaches depravity and degradation at the expense of mutual pleasure and intimacy.

Is it *possible* for pornography to resemble an act of mutual, committed love? Of course, but don't even think about using that as an excuse to dismiss this point. Any honest assessment of pornography must acknowledge that it has no intention of limiting itself to such quasi-legitimate depictions. Why? Because pornography is also progressive.

Progressive This is the very nature of sin, isn't it? Sin is always progressive, and Sheol is never satisfied

(Proverbs 27:20). It always wants more. It always seeks to break out beyond its current boundaries. If you give it an inch, it soon seeks to take a mile.

Have you ever been scared by the progressive nature of your sin? Perhaps there was a time when you saw how a particular sin was taking you over. You had thought you were in control of your sin but then, almost in an instant, you found it had jumped to the next level. You were no longer in control—sin was leading the way and you were more and more just along for the ride, obeying the impulses of the flesh. It's a terrifying place to be, isn't it?

I know beyond doubt that many, many young men (middle-aged and older men, as well) can testify to pornography's power to take control, one level after another. A man's first glimpse of porn may be fleeting—intriguing but short-lived. A naked body is all the eye needs, and a single glimpse provides plenty of fuel for a while. But before long the heart craves more. What was once satisfying is now boring; what was once gross is suddenly desirable. Along the way, a person's whole perception of sex is changed. No longer does sex involve simple intercourse between a man and a woman. Instead it becomes a series of acts, even acts that are in some ways uncomfortable or degrading.

If you have been looking at porn for any length of time, I know you can identify with this. Certain things that interested you at the beginning, that got you going, now seem pretty bland. And things that were once gross are already beginning to intrigue you. This is the way sin is. This is the way sin *always* is. It will always demand more of you. And meanwhile, as you have been more or less certain that you've been controlling your sin, it has actually been controlling you. Subtly, unrelentingly, it has reshaped your mind and your heart in very real ways.

That's why you need a reset. A return to normal. A detox.

Clarifying the Promises

The first message of this book, then, is that you must see what porn is doing to your heart. You must recognize that the corruption of pornography is real and, despite the convenient and self-indulgent little lies we can tell ourselves, that corruption is only going to get worse. The sin underlying the consumption of pornography will not stop escalating until it cripples your marriage, or until you die, or until you get too old and weak to care about sex. The only difference for single guys? The sin won't stop escalating until it destroys any hope you will ever get married.

I want you to hate and fear the realities of pornography as you ought to hate and fear the sin itself. I want you to know that you cannot be a loving husband, an effective husband, or a godly man as long as your mind is filled with the lies of pornography.

I want you to see that you *do* need to quit looking at porn, and (even if you've already broken free) that you need to find a new way of looking at sex. This is because the detox comes in two parts. This two-step process is familiar to anyone who has studied what the Bible calls sanctification: there is the *putting off* of old ways and the *putting on* of new — the rejection of pornography and the embrace of a godly view of sexuality.

So, what's the goal? We need to be clear about where we are trying to go. We need expectations that make sense in two ways. First, our expectations must be neither lower nor higher than the realities we see in Scripture. Second, our expectations must be in keeping with what's possible in a short book like this.

First, remember that we are trying to reset or detox back to a time when porn had little or no hold on you. You cannot be reset to a state of sinlessness, because you were never there! You and I will always be susceptible to temptation. No program can deliver from the *experience* of sexual temptation. And no plan, program, or discipline can guarantee that you will never *give in* to temptation.

Huge, wonderful progress can indeed be made. When this book talks about being "set free" from sexual sin, that's what it's saying. God wants us to make that kind of remarkable progress, he's eager to give us the grace to do it, and we should strive for it with every fiber of our being. But this is not about perfection. Therefore, stumbles and struggles do not equal failure. When properly handled, they are simply part of the progress.

Second, my expertise is limited and this book is short. All I can do here is try to frame the issue for you clearly, inspire you to take it seriously, and offer you a simple path and some next steps based on scriptural teaching. At the end of the day, I want you to take ownership of this issue in your own life. If you do that—if you take seriously the directives and suggestions in this book, and cry out to God for grace to implement them and be shown additional steps—you can have every confidence that God will be pleased to hear and help you.

Think

I'm going to end each chapter with a Think section. Especially in this rapid-fire digital age, it's far too easy to zip through information we truly need and then skip on to the next chunk of information, without ever really reflecting on what we've only halfway absorbed.

Pornography is an area where it's especially important to be honest. Whether you use these questions in a group discussion, or just by yourself, I've put them here to help you take a moment to reflect and, hopefully, to get very real about this.

1. Let's get this one out of the way up-front. Have you ever seen pornography? Yes or no?

2. That was a pretty simple question, so let's ramp it up a bit. How did you first see pornography and how old were you? How many times have you seen it since?

3. When was the last time that you saw pornography? Did "it find you" or did you go looking for it?

4. Have you ever been frightened by your sin? When? How did you react?

5. Have you found that the things in pornography that interested you or excited you at first continue to interest and excite you? Or have your tastes changed? Be honest.

6. Do you think that your mind, your heart, or your expectations of your wife (if you're married) or your perception of women in general (if you're not married) have been affected by pornography? In what manner?

7. If you're married, do you think that pornography has affected your mind, your heart or your expectations of your wife? How, specifically?

Two
PORNOGRAPHY VS. MARRIAGE

By now, it may not surprise you to learn that when I meet a young man, even a young husband, I pretty much assume he either *is* or *was* into pornography. I honestly don't think that's unrealistic, unfair, or cynical. It's the accessibility problem again. Porn is so prevalent that it's nearly certain every young man will find it; and once it has been tasted, it is difficult not to indulge.

Then, as they say, life eventually imitates "art." A young man enters into marriage with his mind full of pornographic images and his heart filled with the abstractions and deceptions of pornographic fantasies. Having seen dozens (hundreds? thousands?) of sex acts in a pornographic setting, he loads the perverse baggage of porn-star expectations onto his wife. The young husband more or less assumes his wife will commit any sexual act he can think of, and that she will do it as gladly, as eagerly, and as skillfully (if that's the right word) as the women he has seen on the screen.

Let's be clear. Porn works its way into your heart in seed form and then seeks to grow as large as possible and take over as much of you as it can. In the process, it crowds out your ability to relate closely to others, especially and most harmfully, your wife. Pornography has unique power to damage a marriage because it is ultimately about self, not union. Indulging in pornography is a form of psychological isolation, a withdrawal into a tiny world of self-gratification. It is a kind of sexual expression that makes your appetites much larger even as your world gets much smaller.

In the previous chapter I said that pornography is inherently violent. We see here the violence that pornography does to human nature as God designed it. Pornography is a representation of sexuality that promotes either isolating acts of masturbation or abhorrently selfish acts of sexual abuse. What it mocks and rejects is a truly intimate joining, the most profound joining a man and woman can know. One of the most deeply harmful things pornography does, therefore, is reinforce the false lesson that sexual excitement is not about a whole-person union at all. Instead, sexual excitement becomes associated with isolation from others and a focus on self. That which is supposed to be about sharing becomes all about getting.

To give yourself over to pornography is to have your whole perception of sexuality altered, shaped by professional pornographers. You—the man whom God has called to love your wife as Christ loves the church—can be looking at her through the eyes of a pornographer! Would you want Hugh Hefner or some Internet porn-video producer staring at your wife's body, looking it up and down, evaluating her by a set of standards that are literally damnable? And yet there you are looking at her through eyes that men like these have given you. You have handed them your sight. You have handed them a piece of your soul. And they have returned your soul to you battered and filthy, and your sight fractured and distorted

So my primary concern with young married men today (more a concern for their wives, or their future wives in the case of single men) is that they may pornify the marriage bed, bringing a foul pollution to that which God intends to be pure, and a rank selfishness to that which God intends to be selfless.

Marriage is No Solution

I've spoken to young single men who think that the answer to their reliance on pornography and their addiction to masturbation is marriage. "If I just get married, I can have legitimate sex and all this sin will just go away." Give the guy a legitimate outlet for his desires and he will no longer seek out the illegitimate, right? This may seem a logical assumption but it is tragically flawed. Legions of men and their hurting wives will testify that it does not work this way at all. Maybe you can testify to it yourself.

Yes, when you marry you may find that at the beginning your relationship with your wife is sexually fulfilling in every way. But sin is almost certainly lying dormant, crouching at the door, awaiting an opportune moment. It may take weeks or months or even years. But sooner or later it will rear its ugly head once again. It may happen when your wife travels for a few days or when you find yourself alone in a hotel room in a strange city. Perhaps it will follow the birth of a baby when for a time your wife is unable to have sex. But at some point it is very likely that the sin will come back to haunt you and to hurt both you and your wife.

What's often overlooked here is that pornography and God-honoring sex within marriage are completely different things. The "marriage will fix everything" idea assumes a measure of equality between illegitimate, selfish sex and legitimate sex within marriage. It assumes bad behavior can simply be replaced with good behavior, traded out like parts on a machine, as if sex were nothing but a mechanical activity. As God makes very clear in his word, sex and the issues surrounding it are fundamentally spiritual in nature. The temptations of pornography engage our minds and bodies in what is primarily a spiritual battle. This battle *includes* a physical component, but it is much *more* than that.

Being tempted to masturbate is probably the most common illegitimate physical expression of this spiritual battle. But that temptation will not end simply because you have a legitimate physical sexual outlet in the person of your wife. The physical battle is not the core issue. It's an outward expression of how well you have been fighting the inner, spiritual battle. "What comes out of the mouth proceeds from the heart, and this defiles a person. For out of the heart come evil thoughts, murder, adultery, sexual immorality, theft, false witness, slander. These are what defile a person" (Matthew 5:18-20).

The external is just an expression of the internal. That's why "replacing" masturbation with the marriage bed can never completely work. There needs to be more than a replacement of the physical, mechanical part of sex. There needs to be a replacement of the spiritual part. In the same way, just quitting porn, while it is the right thing to do, is not enough. As in all matters of spiritual growth, you need to replace lies with truth, and an unholy practice with a holy one.

One more thing. I said this in the previous chapter, and I'll probably say it again. No matter how mature you get in this area, the battle doesn't end. Yes, detox is real. It's needed, it's critical, it's an absolute must-have. But it's no magic bullet or stake in the heart of your sin. Think of the purest, most noble, most mature Christian man you know. He is probably far more immune to porn's enticements than most guys, but he is not completely immune. Neither will you be. Ever.

The wonderful transformation of a deep and thorough detox is necessary. Then, you *will* be stronger. There *will* be a new lightness and sense of freedom and joy in God as he pours out fresh grace. But none of us ever "arrive" in any kind of permanent way. We never become immune to this parasite of the soul.

So, g*etting* free and *staying* free are different things but they involve the same process: Repentance, putting off the old, and putting on the new. You need to practice all three, on a regular basis, for the rest of your life. Sorry. That's how it is.

The next two chapters are on the theology of sexuality so we're on the same page, then the detox part. But first:

Think

1. Do you believe that pornography has done something to your heart? How would you describe that in your own words?

2. Before you were married, (if you are…), did you ever find yourself thinking that your problem with pornography and masturbation would just go away if only you were married? Did it?

3. Do you believe that masturbation and pornography are bad for marriage? In what ways?

4. Do you believe that masturbation and pornography tend to make you more open and joyful with people in general, or more secretive and isolated?

5. When it comes to sexual sin, are you more committed to your sin or to obeying God? Seriously.

Three
A THEOLOGY OF MASTURBATION

When I was a child, wild rumors about the physical effects of masturbation were rampant among my peers. Who knows how the rumors got started, but we whispered back and forth to each other, with all the authority schoolboys can muster, that people who did it grew hair on their palms, lost hair on their heads, went blind, or just went crazy. But as James Dobson has said, "If it did [cause such afflictions], the entire male population and about half of females would be blind, weak, simpleminded and sick. Between 95 and 98 percent of all boys engage in this practice—and the rest have been known to lie." My parents certainly never told me fables about masturbation. Neither did my teachers or youth leaders. But on the playground the stories were alive and well. We may not have been very clear on what sexual intercourse was, or where babies came from, but we were pretty sure we knew what would happen if we masturbated...too much.

Doesn't the persistence of these rumors reveal something obvious? Masturbation is a source of guilt and shame. People who practice it worry they will be exposed. Yet those rumors from my childhood are unfounded. You don't actually go blind or lose your hair. There is no *physical* reason to deny oneself this quasi-sexual pleasure. Then, where does the guilt and shame come from? Is it just an irrational psychological hang-up? Is masturbation actually wrong?

This is a really important question. I'm taking this time to discuss masturbation for two reasons. First, because it afflicts almost all men. And second, because if we get this subject wrong, we get our whole theology of sex wrong. So let's begin by asking a couple of prominent Christian writers who aren't so sure masturbation is sinful.

In his book, *When Good Men Are Tempted*, author Bill Perkins writes, "It appears to me that masturbation is amoral. Under some circumstances it's acceptable behavior. On other occasions it's clearly wrong." He goes on to provide three tests he says will gauge whether a particular instance is right or wrong: the thought test (whether the act is accompanied by inappropriate fantasies), the self-control test (whether the act becomes obsessive), and the love test (whether it leads to a person failing to fulfill the needs of his spouse).

James Dobson teaches a similar view. When I

was young, my parents gave me his book *Preparing for Adolescence*, and I remember well its claims about masturbation. Dobson says essentially that every boy tries masturbation, and he believes that the guilt it creates wreaks havoc on the consciences of countless young children. He says parents should rarely speak to their children about masturbation, but if they do, they should reassure their children that such practices are normal. Here is what he says on his website:

> It is my opinion that masturbation is not much of an issue with God. It is a normal part of adolescence that involves no one else. It does not cause disease. It does not produce babies, and Jesus did not mention it in the Bible. I'm not telling you to masturbate, and I hope you won't feel the need for it. But if you do, it is my opinion that you should not struggle with guilt over it. Why do I tell you this? Because I deal with so many Christian young people who are torn apart with guilt over masturbation; they want to stop and just can't. I would like to help you avoid that agony.

I am quite sure that Dr. Dobson has nothing but good intentions, and while I know less about Bill Perkins, I am willing to extend to him the same good will. But I do need to take a moment to critique their general perspective on this subject.

The Perkins Test

Just a few quick comments on the test that author Bill Perkins offers. He says masturbation is wrong if any one of three things is true. But not one part of his test stands up to even the slightest biblical scrutiny.

First, he says masturbation is wrong if it is accompanied by inappropriate fantasies. For a man, however, the only appropriate sexual fantasy is one involving his wife. And if this leads to masturbation, as I will discuss later, maintaining control of the fantasy to keep it focused on one's wife is close to impossible.

Second, he says masturbation is wrong if it becomes obsessive. But the Bible doesn't require a failure of self-control to be obsessive before it becomes sin. Certainly, a pattern of sin is worse than an instance of sin, but both are wrong.

Third, he says masturbation is wrong if it leads to a person failing to fulfill the needs of his spouse. A prolonged physical separation between husband and wife could certainly produce a situation where masturbation would not rob sexual enjoyment from a spouse. But obviously, that is not the only criterion. There are no grounds for concluding that masturbation is allowed simply because you won't see your wife again for a long time.

Condemned Without Being Named

Dr. Dobson, for his part, says that masturbation is a normal part of adolescence. *Normal* is an interesting word, isn't it? In this context it's comforting, almost wholesome. But *normal* is not a synonym for morally acceptable. If all have sinned and fall short of the glory of God, then sin is both absolutely normal and horribly wrong. None of us get off the hook because "everybody does it" and therefore (big sigh of relief) we're just normal.

To be honest, Dobson's statement here is very nearly humanistic. He sees that masturbation is extremely common. He sees that the natural response to it is guilt and shame. So he concludes that the guilt and shame must be unfounded.

Neither Dobson nor Perkins makes an effort to look carefully at what Scripture says about this topic. They do have a conclusion, though. They say that masturbation is amoral, neither good nor bad in itself. Why? Because no Bible passage specifically allows or condemns it by name. I'm not ascribing the following words to either of the authors I've mentioned, but on a website that takes this general view I recently read: "If masturbation is a sin, then it's a little odd that Scripture would leave the believer guessing about its moral status."

But the Bible is not silent on this subject. It

does not leave us guessing. It's true that Scripture never mentions masturbation specifically. However, because the Bible *does* speak thoroughly and explicitly about sexuality and sinful lust, it *doesn't have to* speak explicitly about something so closely related as masturbation.

Let's look at two ways we can know that the Bible condemns masturbation without ever naming it.

First, consider that if masturbation is extremely common (as are most sins), and nearly always associated with sinful lust, we can safely assume the same was true in the ancient world. So think of Jesus delivering the Sermon on the Mount. When he essentially said "to imagine having sex with a woman is a kind of adultery" (Matthew 5:28), do you think that maybe—just maybe—the men in the audience understood that masturbation was part of his point?

Second, consider that the Bible never refers directly to abortion. Yet, because Scripture speaks clearly about the value of human life and the sin of murder, we are right to conclude that abortion is sin. In almost precisely the same way, because Scripture speaks clearly about the power of sexuality and the sin of lust, we can conclude that masturbation is nearly always sinful. In each case the specific action is so closely linked to the larger category of sin that the connection and shared moral status are simply obvious.

Technically, it *is* accurate to say that masturbation is amoral: You can't say it is *always* bad or *always* good. This is because on very rare occasions masturbation may not be sinful. But the same is true of abortion. In rare, extreme cases, taking the life of an unborn child may be the best course of action: if a fetus is allowed to continue developing within a woman's fallopian tube, for example, both the baby and mother will die. But the rare exception does not and should not stop us from confidently asserting the general rule that the Bible teaches abortion is sinful. So let's not hesitate to say this, either: The Bible teaches that masturbation is sinful.

The Damage Done

Why, exactly, is masturbation sinful? Most importantly, just like any other sin, because it violates God's holiness. Masturbation is against God, against his ways and his purposes for how men and women are to relate to one another in a marital union that reflects the relationship of Christ to the Church.

Masturbation is also sinful because it compromises us. We are made in God's image. We are meant to glorify him in every aspect of our lives, and masturbation hinders us in this mission in two principal ways: by polluting our minds and by inclining us to isolation.

Mind Pollution

Sexual gratification, of course, is not just a physical act, but one that engages the mind, often quite intensely. During male masturbation, pornographic images, whether seen externally or visualized internally, nearly always provide the fuel. Indeed, the vast majority of the time, these image-based fantasies are nearly impossible to separate from the masturbation itself. This type of fantasy can be dangerous in at least two ways.

First, as most adults have learned the hard way, reality is rarely as wonderful as fantasy. Many people create expectations for sex that reality cannot meet. I dare say that rarely has a teenage boy created a fantasy in which his partner rebuffs his advances because she is too tired. Neither has he concocted a fantasy in which she declines participation in a particular act because she finds it uncomfortable or distasteful. The fact is that fantasy can form unhealthy and unrealistic expectations of sex.

Second, just as sex scenes in movies rarely involve married couples who can, before God, legitimately enjoy sex, fantasy rarely revolves around legitimate sex partners. In theory, it is fine for a husband to dream of a sexual encounter with his wife, but after that things get tricky. Masturbation, even under those circumstances, may encourage the best husband to fill his mind with thoughts of other women. And a single Christian man, having no God-given partner with whom he can consummate sexual desire, simply has no legitimate reason for pursuing sexual fantasy at all.

Some will protest that when they masturbate it is merely a physical act, something done to relieve stress or boredom. They will insist that they do not succumb to thinking inappropriate thoughts. I am extremely skeptical of these claims, but I do not dismiss them, because I cannot see into anyone else's heart or read anyone else's mind. But even assuming, for the sake of argument, that a small proportion of men masturbate without any pornographic images in their heads, there is still at least one powerful reason why masturbation is so harmful.

Isolation

A close examination of the Bible's teaching on sexuality uncovers no reason to believe that God ever intended sex to be a private pursuit. Indeed, the heart and soul of sexuality is the giving and receiving of sexual pleasure between two people: one husband and one wife.

Sex is intended to be a means of mutual fulfillment, an expression of love in which a husband thinks foremost of his wife, and the wife thinks foremost of her husband. It is a uniquely powerful means by which husband and wife can fulfill the Lord's command to esteem another higher than oneself. As they fulfill each other's needs, they also have their own needs fulfilled. It is a beautiful picture of intimacy! As any married couple can testify, the more selfless the sex, the better sex becomes. The more each spouse seeks to please the other, the more fulfilling, gratifying, and beautiful the experience.

This mutual giving and receiving, the heart of God's purpose for sexuality, is exactly what masturbation does not and cannot provide. Masturbation strips sexuality of its divine purpose of mutual fulfillment. Where legitimate sexual expression is meant to produce unity, masturbation produces isolation and division. As we saw in Chapter 2 when discussing pornography, masturbation is inherently self-centered. Together, pornography and masturbation create a fictitious sense of intimacy between the viewer and some anonymous person in a magazine or on a screen. But an act that can seem like it's about two people is completely and exclusively about one person, all alone. Masturbation (again, even in the hypothetical absence of pornographic imagery) deeply undermines a man's ability to deny and resist his most self-centered, sinful, isolationist tendencies.

Masturbation simply cannot fulfill God's design for sexuality, and thus has no place in the life of one who calls himself a Christian.

Handling the Guilt

But what about the guilt? What about the shame and fear that makes young boys imagine hair sprouting on the palms of their hands? Should we try to just sweep the guilt away? Is masturbation something parents should tell children not to be troubled about. . . because it's "normal"? In the name of preserving us from pain, this kind of advice teaches us to ignore our moral conscience. Better to warp our souls, it seems, than to stress our psyches.

Speak honestly and openly to young people, however, and they *do* want to talk about their struggles with masturbation. They do want to be reassured that it is wrong and that they can and must overcome it. The guilt they feel is not irrational, but a manifestation of God's grace. Like a nerve ending that tells you to take a stone out of your shoe before you begin to bleed, such guilt is pain with a corrective purpose.

It's important to clarify what we should be guilty about in the first place. (As John Piper might say, "Don't waste your guilt!") Masturbation is obviously a very graphic act, so it can be natural to focus on that act as the essential problem. Men generally feel bad *because* they have masturbated (or been strongly tempted to). But masturbation is really only an outward *manifestation* of an inner problem. There is guilt and emotional pain and a sense of being dirty within, because the act of masturbation has revealed the corruption continually dwelling within us. Yes, the act of masturbation is wrong in and of itself, as reflected in Paul's command to cultivate self-control. But the only reason it happens to begin with is because of indwelling sin.

As Josh Harris writes in *Sex Is Not The Problem (Lust Is)*, "masturbation isn't a filthy habit that makes people dirty. It only reveals the dirt that's already in our hearts." So while masturbation does not *make* anyone filthy, it does take a mental and spiritual toll as guys struggle with feelings of guilt, remorse, and shame. Unfortunately, for most of us, guilt alone is not enough to curb our sinful behaviors.

Sadly, though, for many Christian men, guilt over masturbation can become so extreme that it begins to define their spiritual state. Some even begin to question their salvation, seeing themselves exclusively through the lens of this persistent sin. There is no doubt this is a serious sin, but it does not begin to deserve such prominence. "When we inflate the importance of this act," Josh Harris writes wisely, "we'll either overlook the many evidences of God's work in us or we'll ignore other more serious expressions of lust that God wants us to address."

If you struggle with this sin, know for certain that there is hope for you, hope for real change. Do not seek reassurance in the cold comfort that "everyone does it." The way to avoid the agony of guilt is not to ignore sin, or make some vain effort to convince yourself it's innocuous. The solution to guilt is to focus on the finished work of Christ on the cross. Take comfort in the good news of the gospel. The blood of Jesus was shed for sins like this one, and the power of the Holy Spirit has been given to us so that we can overcome sin. Masturbation is not a sin beyond the power of God. You *can* be set free.

Think

1. Though masturbation does not bring about bad physical effects, many guys who masturbate still wrestle with guilt and sadness. Can you identify with this? If you have masturbated in the past, did you experience feelings of guilt?
2. Is it possible to have a sinless mind even while masturbating? Is there an argument to be made that the physical act is harmless and that it is only the accompanying fantasies that are wrong?
3. Do you understand why masturbation can be referred to as "self-centered sex" or "selfish sex?" In what ways does the solo nature of masturbation go against God's plan for sex?
4. The Bible tells us that a man's body belongs to his wife. How does this impact the discussion on masturbation? Does it leave you with the right to

perform any sexual deeds apart from your wife?

5. Do you want to stop masturbating? Or is it a sin you enjoy so much that you would be very disappointed and unwilling to give it up?

6. Do you believe that Christ is willing to forgive you for this sin and that, through his Holy Spirit, he is both willing and able to free you from it?

Four
THREE GIFTS OF SEX

When God created man, he created him male and female. At least, when God created the *idea* of man, he created him male and female and commanded him to be fruitful and to multiply, to subdue and rule the rest of creation. But when God actually breathed life into the dust of the ground and formed a living, breathing human being, he created just one person, one man: Adam, the first and for a time the only human. Male and female had been created in the mind of God, but so far only this one man walked upon the earth.

We do not know how long it was before God formed Eve, but we do know that for a time, Adam lived a life of celibacy. And during this time, he joined with God in the search for a suitable mate. God said, "It is not good that the man should be alone; I will make him a helper fit for him" (Genesis 2:18). And yet he did not make this helper immediately. Instead, he brought before Adam every living creature, one by one. And in all of creation there was no helper for Adam, no mate suitable to him. Through all this time Adam waited patiently, he waited perfectly, sinlessly trusting in God's provision. Was Eden flawed in the absence of sex and marriage? Not at all! It would just be better *with* them for, in the words of God, for it was not good for this man to be alone.

When Adam finally saw his wife, he broke into a song of praise, saying:

> *This at last is bone of my bones*
> *and flesh of my flesh;*
> *she shall be called Woman,*
> *because she was taken out of Man.*

Do not neglect the words "at last." It was through that period of searching, that period of sinless waiting on God, that Adam learned to appreciate what God ultimately provided. It was in his innocence that Adam could best appreciate God's grace.

When Eve arrived, so did the unique relationship we now call marriage. Adam's period of celibacy was over, its purpose accomplished; the opportunity for sexual intimacy was at hand. And it was a good thing. A very good thing. Under the right conditions, it still is.

Sex is Good

Many theologians have attempted to get at the deepest meaning of sex. "Sex is a picture, a metaphor, to point us to the joys of heaven," they might say. And perhaps this is so. But I don't find that the Bible tells us this clearly. Neither am I convinced that we need to find some deeper meaning in sex in order to affirm its goodness. Sex is inherently good because it was created by a good God. We do not need to construct a complex theology around sex, as if it is only good in some secondary sense.

Sex within marriage is perfectly good in and of itself. Even if its ultimate meaning is no deeper than pleasure and mutual fulfillment, it is good because God is good. He could easily have decreed that sex be an integral part of every marriage and then made it inherently unpleasant! He did not. He made sex almost transcendent in its pleasure. At its best, sex really does surpass most of life's other pleasures in its joy, freedom, and vulnerability. And in these things, sex draws a husband and wife together in a completely unique and unparalleled way.

When you understand this—that sex has the power to unite two people in ways nothing else does—you will also understand why sex is meant to be enjoyed only between a husband and wife. You will understand why God forbids pre-marital sex (fornication), why he forbids extra-marital sex (adultery), and why he even forbids selfish sex (masturbation). All these things make a mockery of the real thing. All these things abuse his good gift.

But let's get a little more specific about why sex is such a good thing. There are at least three ways in which sex encourages and affirms the good: sex motivates joyful obedience, it strengthens male leadership, and it enhances true freedom.

Sex Motivates Joyful Obedience

Some say that sexual desire is meant only to motivate procreation—that the desire to have sex will draw a husband and wife together with the happy and ultimate result of conception. Here C.S. Lewis applies a helpful corrective (in *Mere Christianity*). He affirms that the biological purpose of sex is procreation (and let's not lose sight of this important purpose to sex) but draws a helpful parallel to the appetite for food.

The biological purpose of eating is to repair the Body, and though some people are given to overindulgence, we find that the appetite goes only a little way beyond its biological purpose. A man may eat twice as much food as his body needs for its biological purpose, but few will eat even that much. When it comes to sex, though, the appetite far exceeds its biological purpose. If the sexual appetite matched its biological function either a person would only desire sex a few times in a lifetime or he would have thousands of children. Does this not teach us that God desires that we have sex for reasons beyond procreation? The only other alternative is that this appetite is a product of sin and ought to be suppressed. But no, this cannot be. The Bible is clear that legitimate sexual desire, desire within a marriage and a desire for one's spouse, is legitimate before God.

God gives a man sexual desire, a sexual appetite, because he wants him to have sex with his wife. Can't it be just that simple? What's more, this appetite surpasses any biological purpose because he wants the couple to have sex *a lot*. After all, the only admonition in Scripture regarding the frequency of married sex appears in 1 Corinthians 7:5, which says there may be a brief pause for specific, limited purposes. The implication is that, otherwise, sex is going to be a normal part of life. In fact, the Bible goes so far as to say that a wife's body *belongs* to her husband—that he has authority over her body—and a husband's body *belongs* to his wife—she has authority over his body. The ruling principle is that husbands and wives are to have sex often, and are not to refuse one another this special gift.

It's good that we want to have sex. God made it that way. God made sex for marriage and marriage for sex. Sexual desire motivates a man (in part) to pursue a wife and marry her so that together they can enjoy sex. This same desire motivates a man (in part) to keep pursuing his wife even after they are married. Without this desire, this appetite, it would be far easier for us to avoid carrying out our God-given duty to have sex, and lots of it, and thus to experience intimacy and unity, and lots of it.

Do you see the beauty and goodness in this? God gives a desire that is meant to be fulfilled in only one way. If we did not experience hunger we might not eat. If we stop eating for too long, we will suffer from a lack of nourishment, our bodies will stop repairing themselves, and we will waste away and begin to die. If we did not experience sexual desire we might not have sex. And if we stop having sex by choice, our marriages will suffer from a lack of intimacy, and similarly slide toward relational death.

Sexual desire, then, is a gift of God, not to torment us but to motivate our obedience. When a husband inevitably feels sexual desire it is not an invitation to pornography and masturbation, but a nudge toward pursuing his wife.

Sex Strengthens A Husband's Leadership

Yet sexual desire, the appetite for sex, is not given in equal measure. It is typically given in greater part to men. Why is this? The answer, I'm convinced, goes right to the heart of the husband-wife relationship.

God commands that men, husbands, be leaders. Men are to take the leading role while women are to follow. God intends that men take leadership even in sex, and, therefore, he gives men a greater desire for sex. This way a man can lead his wife, taking the initiative, taking care to love her so as to draw her toward wanting to have sex with him.

I am under the impression that the Fall happened fairly soon after Creation. How much time came between the two events is not clear. But we can assume that during that time, in that perfect world, Adam and Eve enjoyed perfect sex. In that interim, there was never an occasion when Eve refused Adam, because there was never a time when Adam was not thinking first of Eve. What reason would she have to refuse? But after they sinned—when Adam stopped thinking first of Eve and when she began to rebel against his leadership—this is when sex became a struggle. And it remains a struggle today. Most husbands and wives will testify that they have had more fights and disagreements about sex than just about anything else. The most special means of grace to a husband and wife has become the greatest cause of strife.

Generally speaking, a man finds intimacy and acceptance *through* sex while a woman needs to first experience intimacy and acceptance *before* she can be prepared to enjoy sex. Most often, this is where the problem arises. How are a husband and wife to navigate this partial mismatch of desires? By understanding the role of godly leadership in marriage and allowing it to work as God intends.

It all begins with a powerful combination: a man's sexual appetite, plus his love for his wife, plus the sexual liberties granted them by virtue of marriage. These are wonderful things, but if they are all the husband sees, he will end up being a sexual bully toward the woman God has given him to love and cherish. He needs to recognize (and learn to navigate) the differences in how he and his wife experience intimacy and acceptance.

A husband's first responsibility is to provide for his wife's needs for intimacy and acceptance *prior* to sex—by romancing her. A wife's corresponding responsibility is to receive her husband's attempts at romance graciously, even when they have not been perfectly executed. (And the husband, in turn, must be gracious toward his wife if she struggles to receive his flawed attempts at romance!)

The husband must seek to lead in such a way that his wife will have no reason to refuse him. He must be sensitive to her needs, to her desires. He must acknowledge the times where, for one reason or another, she would find it exceedingly difficult to give herself to him. And he must not cajole her into acts that would make her uncomfortable or leave her feeling violated. He needs to exemplify leadership as a servant, even in the bedroom. His first thoughts must be for her.

As in all areas of life, a wife is called to defy her husband's leadership only if he demands of her something that would violate her conscience or God's law. We can see this as a reactive responsibility of the wife, but more importantly it is a proactive responsibility of the husband. That is, in exercising his leadership, the husband is never to put his wife in a situation where she has to appeal to her conscience or the Bible in the face of her husband's sexual desires.

So, a husband's sexual appetite cannot be separated from his leadership. The husband has a desire that only his wife can meet. Therefore, he takes the lead in seeking to fulfill that desire. He does this by meeting the desires of his wife that will, in turn, cause her to see and appreciate and eventually fulfill his desires. And then, in that act of consummation, God grants a grace that surpasses the mere union of flesh and blood.

Sex Enhances True Freedom

Finally, God gives us sex because it has unique power in drawing a husband to his wife and a wife to her husband. Sex is intended by God to be alluring and even captivating. It is meant to put a powerful emotional seal on *marriage* — not on masturbation, or fornication, or any other sinful use of sex. That kind of sinful captivation is bondage, and has guilt and shame woven into it. But within marriage the captivation inherent in the sexual relationship is freedom, and has joy and gratitude woven in.

Through sexual union a husband and wife are made one, gloriously bound together. There is a mystery to it that can only be compared to the union of God and his people as they are grafted into him. In the gift of sexual intimacy, God gives husband and wife something remarkably powerful. He was wise to place strict boundaries on such power, and he has every right to do so, because he is the one who created sex and gave it its marvelous, unifying, captivating purpose.

- Sex, then, is to be shared only between a husband and a wife, and cannot be extended to others either before marriage or during marriage (Matthew 5:27-28). To introduce anyone else into the relationship, whether physically or even abstractly, such as through shared pornography, is a perversion of the one-to-one nature of sexuality.
- Sex, as with everything else in life, is to be done with self-control, not with recklessness or self-indulgence. This means sex is to be done in love, not anger. Tragically, a man can rape his own

wife if he violently forces himself upon her. What a violation of sex this is!

- Sex must not be stirred up or awakened until the time is right (Song of Solomon 8:4).
- Sex is to be practiced regularly throughout a marriage (1 Corinthians 7:1-5).

What is the underlying point and purpose of these boundaries? Like everything else God gives, they are for our good. In fact, in keeping with God's design for sex, these boundaries encourage, enforce, and enhance freedom. Not the world's view of freedom, which is more a kind of untethered, borderless anarchy, but sexual freedom as God designed it. True freedom.

God's boundaries, rightly observed, do not inhibit freedom, but enhance it. When we try to pursue freedom as we choose to define it, we suffer. Like foolish children who don't know the difference between freedom and mortal danger, we run toward the traffic and can't imagine why anyone would start screaming. But when we use the gift of sex as God intends, we gain great joy and freedom in it. God's boundaries make true freedom possible.

So, sex is a good thing, marvelously good. And the boundaries God has established for it are good as well. Now, on to the detox.

Think

1. In your own words, describe the purposes for which God created sex. Before reading this, had you ever thought about why he saw fit to create it?

2. Do you believe God can create pleasurable things simply because he delights in the pleasure they bring to us? What examples, other than sex, can you think of?

3. Have you ever been frustrated or angry with God about the fact that he has given you sexual desire?

4. What message is sexual desire sending you? To answer that, you must first answer: What is the purpose of sexual desire in your life? And the answer to that depends on whether you are single or married!

5. In what ways does pornography make a mockery of God's intention for sex?

6. Do you believe that God can give you what you need to completely refrain from sexual sin?

Five
DETOX IN THE BEDROOM

Now that we have a basic biblical understanding of the goodness of sex and the sexual boundaries God has established, we should ask, *How should a husband best express his love for his wife sexually?* This kind of big-picture question is vitally important. We can get in trouble, however, if we then pursue the next question that's likely to come to mind: *Which things are okay to do, and which are not?* Most guys want to move quickly from the abstract to the concrete, from the general to the specific. Principles aren't good enough. We want a checklist. *What should I do in bed? What should I not do?*

I could certainly draw up a checklist for you—lots of boxes representing particular sex acts, each box containing a confidence-boosting check mark or a big, discouraging X. It would probably feel very organized, and in some ways it might even be helpful. The problem is that it would be *my* list, and I can't give you anything definitive. I can't give you the Bible's list because there isn't one.

Any list I create would inevitably reflect *my* conscience, *my* strengths, and *my* weaknesses. It would almost certainly be legalistic in some ways and licentious in others. The same would be true for any list you or anyone else might write up. What one couple finds blissfully enjoyable is repulsive to another. One person's sexual freedom is another person's unholy captivity, even within the boundaries and liberties of marriage. That is one of the strange realities of the way God has made us—he has made us different and has even given us different consciences.

This means, as we saw in the previous chapter, that there is great freedom within marriage to explore, to try new things, and to enjoy things that are mutually pleasurable. On the question of sexual acts within marriage, the Bible leaves things very general, encouraging husbands and wives to find the patterns and practices consistent with Scripture that work best for them as a couple.

The right approach, therefore, is to ask, *What is God's design for sex? What is his intention?* For an honest Christian couple, this approach will lead to a set of practices that are mutually enjoyable and rewarding and, at the same time, entirely in keeping with Scripture. A long and ultimately disappointing checklist approach is a poor substitute for having a biblical perspective and observing some godly guidelines. In this chapter we'll cover guidelines of both the positive and negative variety.

What Sex is Not

Because of our sin nature, there are at least three things we can all too easily assume sex *is*, when it really *isn't*.

Sex is not ultimate. If your only influence was popular culture you might never realize this, but sex is not the ultimate thing in life. Whether married or single, we can tend to make sex into more than it is. Idols begin as good things to which we give too much importance, and few things slide over into idolatry with greater frequency or greater power than sex. We allow a good gift of God to supersede the God who gave it. Sex is good, and even great, but it's not ultimate.

Sex is not mediated. We are a thoroughly mediated people today. Our technology mediates, or stands in between, us and the physical world. Every year, we experience more and more of life indirectly, through some sort of screen, whether computer, TV, movie, cell phone, or whatever else. We have grown accustomed to learning through screens, communicating through screens, even worshiping through screens. Many have grown accustomed to experiencing sex through them as well.

Through the lens of online pornography, an entire generation is learning a set of half-truths about real sex. Tragically, the first sexual experiences of many, if not most, of today's young people take place in a mediated context where a screen displays the sexual act and the viewer responds. But what is sex supposed to be, really? Sex is meant to be the ultimate in unmediated contact, contact between two real people, two im-mediate people. It is the face-to-face, body-to-body, soul-to-soul nature of sex that makes it so powerful and meaningful. Mediated sex is an oxymoron, a self-contradiction, an activity that has lost its essential power and purpose. It is a fraudulent, counterfeit version of sex. Sex simply cannot exist in a pure, biblical, essential, human way, in a mediated environment. The medium is directly opposed to the purpose.

<u>Sex is not primarily about people.</u> With all the human, physical passions surrounding sex, it can be hard to grasp fully that sex is not primarily about you, or even about your spouse. Sex is about God. Does that sound odd? It's true. A husband may be motivated by a desire to pursue his wife and have sex with her. That's all well and good. But a Christian husband who has embraced a biblical view of sex will be motivated ultimately by obedience to God's command—that a husband and wife are to enjoy sex frequently, honoring God by honoring one another.

A wife may be motivated to have sex by a desire to please her husband or to avoid a fight. That may be fine, too. But if she's thinking biblically, her primary or ultimate motivation will be to obey God.

Imagine that on a particular occasion a married Christian has no desire for sex. Because of God's command, that husband or wife should seriously reconsider. In fact, even if neither spouse wants sex for a prolonged time, the couple should still have sex for God's sake out of obedience to him. (Such a couple also needs to address the larger issue of why the desire for intimacy has slipped away!)

When the subject turns to God's expectations about sex, it can be difficult to hear clearly what's being said (although if it's *really* difficult, that may be a sign that for you sex has become ultimate). Sex *is* rightly a private, sensitive matter, so it can feel odd to have it addressed. But God also has a right to the private aspects of our lives, too. We don't get to keep sex as a little world all our own.

So let's recognize that sex is about God in the same way that our speech is about God, and what we do with our money is about God, and how we spend our free time is about God. In each case God demands primacy, and his standard is nothing less than perfect obedience. So a loving husband and wife who understand the biblical teaching about marriage will sometimes have sex, for God's sake, even when they don't want to—but if they fail in this area, the gospel provides a way for their disobedience to be forgiven, just as with any other sin. As with speech, or money, or employer/employee relations, or anything else, it's not that either you're perfect or you're a hopeless reprobate. It's about understanding that God is first in all things, even sex, and we must seek to obey him by grace.

What Sex Is

We have seen that that the Bible defines God-honoring sex as good, wholesome, true, commanded, and having clear boundaries. We have acknowledged that this creates tremendous freedom in a marriage. It is a freedom to explore, to discover, to play, to say Yes or No or Never Again. But it is a freedom that may need to be sanctified, to be made holy, especially for those who have had their understanding of sex shaped by pornography. We probably all need some detox in the bedroom.

Magazines and advice websites (Christian and non-Christian) are full of questions about what constitutes acceptable sexual behavior. When I read those questions, it is not difficult to know which were written by people whose appetites have been shaped by porn. It's the questions that essentially ask, "Is it okay if my wife and I play out this particular pornographic act?"

We must return to this point: The things that supposedly arouse porn stars are very likely *not* the things that will arouse your wife or make her feel loved and treasured. They are far more likely to make her feel demeaned—turned into some convenient object instead of a precious bride. Set out some of the positive things we see in the Bible about sex, and it's not hard to recognize that pornography demonstrates the opposite.

- Sex is tender. Is there tenderness in pornography? Or violence?
- Sex is sweet. Is there sweetness in pornography? Or degradation?
- Sex is selfless and giving. But again, pornography is all about conquest, about having my most base and selfish needs met. Right now.
- Sex has boundaries. Pornography scoffs at boundaries. It teaches that anything I desire is acceptable merely because I desire it.

Always remember that most pornography is designed to incite lust in a particular kind of person— one already calloused against what is good and pure. Porn is created to arouse the hardened heart, not the tender heart.

The Right Questions

So the question remains. How is a husband to determine what he ought to do with his wife in the bedroom? He has to do *something*. What should he do and not do?

Once we understand that there is no Divine Sex Checklist, and we're clear on some of the things sex *is* and *is not*, we can turn to asking the primary question. We do that, however, by exploring secondary questions. Here are five such secondary questions that I think will prove very helpful. Each one is designed to help you answer from a biblical perspective the age-old question: *Is it okay if I _____?*

What is your heart in this? Any action we take, in the bedroom or anywhere else, is motivated by the heart. So there is more value in asking, "What is in my heart that I *want* to do this?" than, "Is this particular act wrong?" Do you see the change in focus? I consider the act, but then trace the desire for that act to its source: my heart. Again, Jesus taught his disciples that it is what comes from within, not external things, that defile a man (Mark 7: 1-23). All evil, whether adultery or covetousness or sexual immorality, comes from within. You need to cultivate a tender heart by being willing to look into your heart to uncover your motives. Why? So you can do only those things primarily motivated by love for your spouse, avoiding things primarily motivated by any kind of sin.

A word of caution: As Christians who still have indwelling sin, our hearts are messy places. Don't get hung up if you realize your motivations in regard to sex or some particular act are a mix of good and bad. Your motives may never be completely pure. Make your judgment based on what you believe is *primarily* motivating you.

Is this the act of a conqueror or of a servant? You know full well that much of pornography depicts acts of conquest, not acts of love and service. You know that in pornography the pleasure of the man is generally far greater and far more genuine than that of the woman. Do not subject your wife to acts that would make her feel like the means to an end, like she has been conquered instead of loved and nurtured, like she has been defiled instead of treasured and respected.

Does this bring pleasure to one or to both? One purpose of sex is to bring mutual pleasure. At its best, sex allows both spouses to give and receive at the same time and through the same acts. It is unique in that way, and uniquely powerful and fulfilling. There may be times when there is some inequity in the giving and receiving of pleasure, but each spouse should always be seeking greater pleasure for the other, not for him or herself. Do not always pleasure yourself at the expense of your spouse; never commit acts which are pleasurable to one and distasteful to the other.

Does this trouble either your conscience or your spouse's conscience? The conscience is a special gift of God, and one that he commands us to heed (see Titus 1:15, where having a defiled conscience is associated with impurity and unbelief). God gives us all the same law through his Word, but he gives each of us a conscience all our own. We are required to heed this conscience and not to violate it. Do not violate your conscience with regard to certain acts and do not cajole your spouse into violating hers.

Can you thank God for this? It is difficult to thank God for things we have done in violation of law or conscience. When considering particular acts, evaluate whether you would be able to thank God for them. If you couldn't, don't do it.

For many men, these guidelines will be disappointing, for in them you may see that certain porn-fueled fantasies—things you have seen on the screen and held dear and hoped to experience—must go unfulfilled. Much of what is portrayed as normal in pornography is forbidden by God as a sin against him and against your spouse. But if you trust God you can know that he will give you grace, not only to get over it—actually, to get over yourself—but also to find greater pleasure in purer things.

Countless committed couples will affirm that they have found great and growing pleasure in years and decades of what, according to pornography, would be very boring sex. For these godly couples, the years of sex exclusively with one another have proven far more interesting, far more alluring, far more intimate, and far more satisfying than any pleasure they could have found in running wild. Do you trust God that this can be the case for you and your bride?

Think

1. When considering what is permissible in sex, what is the potential risk in focusing on a checklist of acts?
2. This chapter says that the acts you see in pornography are designed to incite lust in the hearts of people who are already hardened against God's true design for sex. Do you believe this is true?
3. Which of the five "right questions" in this chapter do you think create the strongest contrast between godly expressions of sexuality and the acts you have seen in pornography?
4. Which of the five questions made you realize that some of your thoughts and expectations of sex have been influenced by pornography?
5. Do you believe that a lifetime of "normal" sex with a single partner can be more fulfilling and more interesting than acts fueled by pornographic fantasy?

Six

DETOX IN YOUR SOUL

So often in this fallen world, sexual desire becomes a heavy burden. If it is for you, then I know your struggles, because not too many years ago they were mine. As a young man I, like so many others, battled with the inability to express my awakening sexual desire honorably and biblically. I even cried out to God, asking why he would give me such a burden. A few more years and I went from young single man to young husband, fighting (and sometimes not fighting) against lust and pornography and all the rest. For a time these things enticed me and drew me and sought to captivate me.

Today, I can say with joy and gratitude that pornography does not have the power over me it once did. God delivered me from the desire to indulge. So I understand your struggles. But I can also assure you that it is possible to find freedom. Not a freedom that means, "I don't do it even though I really, really want to," but a freedom that means truly not even desiring it anymore. It's gone. God showed me the horror of it, he showed the beauty of purity, and he has graciously taken away the desire to sin in this area.

How is this accomplished? No one has ever devised a better method for overcoming sin than that which God articulated through Paul. Standing firm in the gospel and relying on the grace and power of God to make our efforts effective, we must put off that which is of the flesh and in its place put on that which is of the Spirit.

Sometimes I wish the world were different. I wish that sin wasn't so persistent or so deeply woven into me. I wish there were some other method for overcoming it. Maybe you wish these things, too. But the reality is that we will never get anywhere in defeating our sin if we don't fight. We have to be about the business of putting sin to death. As we approach the end of this book, are you ready for the Great Concluding Insight?

You need to stop looking at pornography. And you need to stop masturbating. Right now. As in, this instant. Not tomorrow. Today.

Will it be difficult? Probably. Will it be the end of the world if you trip up once in a while? Not even close. So then, do you really have to be serious about stopping? Do you have to keep on trying? Yes, you absolutely do.

Ignoring the fact that sexual temptation has its hooks in you just won't work. You cannot simply hide it away out of sight, pretending it's not there. It's like those people you hear about on the news who murder someone and stuff the body into a wall or put it in a box in the basement. Who can imagine this technique might be successful? Before long the body is going to rot and smell. The reality of the situation is going to become obvious all by itself.

This is how sin is. You can try to wall it off and prop something legitimate in front of it. You can box it up and throw a blanket over it. But it's all just an exercise in denial. Sooner or later the death you have tucked away is going to stink. You won't fool anyone in the end, least of all the One who sees to the depths of the heart. "Sheol and Abaddon lie open before the Lord; how much more the hearts of the children of man" (Proverbs 15:11). Do not ignore your sin!

Instead of ignoring our sin, you need to be about the daily business of killing it. And as you kill it, as you put it off, you need to replace lies with truth. You need to begin a program that will help reshape your understanding of sex, replacing the distortions with pure truth. "Put to death therefore what is earthly in you: sexual immorality, impurity, passion, evil desire, and covetousness, which is idolatry. On account of these the wrath of God is coming" (Colossians 3:5-6). God has given you the Bible so

71

you can do just that. Through the Bible we are able to borrow God's eyes, see the world as he sees it, and know what to do about it.

God's Eyes

For me, a handful of Scripture passages became foundational to my understanding of sex, and empowered my self-control. When I was young and considering marriage, and later when I was young and newly married, these passages were instrumental means of grace to me in my determination not to succumb to the allure of pornography. Four passages in particular stood out.

The Laughter of Love

This first verse I want to look at is a bit of a strange one, I admit. Genesis 26:8 involves the story of Isaac and Abimelech, the pagan king of Gerar. You remember that Isaac—like his father, Abraham—traveled through a strange land and feared for his life. Also like his father, Isaac took the coward's way out of a tight spot by denying his wife rather than risking his own welfare. But then Abimelech looked out of a window and "saw Isaac laughing with Rebekah his wife." That word laughing is apparently a difficult one to translate and versions of the Bible render it quite differently. When I was young I read a commentary that said, rightly, it could be translated as "'sporting.'"

Abimelech looked out his window and saw Isaac and Rebekah doing *something* that made him realize they were definitely not brother and sister. At the same time, Abimelech knew Isaac's character well enough not to accuse him of anything immoral. Isaac and Rebekah were sporting—they were playing, flirting, simply enjoying young love (just maybe not in the wisest location). Somehow this passage depicted for me a freedom and innocence I wanted to have with my wife. Two things were very clear to me: I knew I wanted this freedom and openness in our marriage, and I knew we could not have it if either of us were sinning sexually against the other.

The Understanding Way

The second verse is 1 Peter 3:7 which commands, "Husbands, live with your wives in an understanding way, showing honor to the woman as the weaker vessel, since they are heirs with you of the grace of life, so that your prayers may not be hindered." Here I realized that my relationship with my wife had huge spiritual importance. If I am not showing honor to my wife, my own prayers (not hers!) will be hindered.

As the leader of my home I need to keep growing spiritually. In order to do this I must be faithful in prayer. And I can only be faithful in prayer, I learned, if I treat my wife as she deserves to be treated. Were I to give in to lust and porn and all other kinds of sexual sin, I would be devastating my family. I would hardly be the only one who suffers. How could I bring that kind of pain upon the people I love most?

The Fountain of Joy

Next is one of my favorite passages in the whole Bible. Proverbs 5:18-19 says, "Let your fountain be blessed, and rejoice in the wife of your youth, a lovely deer, a graceful doe. Let her breasts fill you at all times with delight; be intoxicated always in her love." I love the sweetness of this passage. It calls a man to find joy, satisfaction, and intimacy always and only in the wife God has given him. It bids him to recall the delight he had in the days when he and his bride were innocent and newly married. And it calls him to live out of that delight. He has no right to go elsewhere, no right to "drink from another cistern," to use Solomon's terminology. And why would he ever want to? The verse celebrates both the gift of sex and its exclusivity.

The Bible calls an unmarried man to be intoxicated with *no* woman. And it calls a married man to be intoxicated, not with just any woman or a series of women, but with *one* woman: the wife of his youth. Every time you look at pornography, every time you give in to lust, you are diminishing your ability to be focused on one woman, intoxicated in her love and finding your joy and satisfaction in her alone.

Just a few verses later come these sobering words. "For a man's ways are before the eyes of the Lord, and he ponders all his paths. The iniquities of the wicked ensnare him, and he is held fast in the cords of his sin. He dies for lack of discipline, and because of his great folly he is led astray." Men who refuse to be intoxicated in the love of their wives, men who find delight in the bodies (or images of the bodies) of other women, are committing acts of great foolishness. This is not a foolishness akin to silliness, but the kind that puts a man in danger of death. It is a moral foolishness that leads to spiritual destruction. Such foolishness, such lack of discipline, such lack of concern for their own sin, diverts men from the path that leads in the direction of moral and spiritual life. This leaves the only other path there is: The path that leads in the direction of moral and spiritual death.

Younger Women as Sisters

The final passage that especially helped me was 1 Timothy 5:1-2, which reads, "Do not rebuke an older man but encourage him as you would a father, younger men as brothers, older women as mothers, younger women as sisters, in all purity." I saw here the connection between the women of pornography and God's command that I treat all young women as sisters. How could I do that if I was leering at them on the screen? How could I leer at anonymous young women on the screen and then assume that I'd be able to then turn off that lust and treat other young women in my life as sisters? Giving in to lust in one area would impact every area. God commanded me to see young women not as sexual objects but as sisters. I had to relate to them with all purity — in my heart, in my mind, in my life.

These verses, though an eclectic collection, challenged me deeply. More than that, they reset my mind. I memorized them, pondered them, called them to mind, and lived by them. Over time, they detoxified my soul. Any desire to pursue sinful lust melted away. I know this was a work of God because he worked through his Word, just as he says he will. In its place he gave me a great and still-growing love for my wife, and increased joy and satisfaction in my relationship with her. I would not want it any other way.

Your Own Secret Weapon

Before concluding, I want to add one more factor to the mix. This has got to be the most unused secret weapon in the church today, and all the more ironic because this "weapon" is an extremely tangible gift from God, a gift presented specifically to help us all grow in holiness.

If you truly want to overcome pornography, talk to your pastor.

Consider all the resources the church has

produced to battle lust and pornography. Consider the hidden-in-plain-sight fact that everyone knows sexual temptation is a huge issue, for nearly every male, for at least part of his life. Why then do we overlook a principal gift from God designed to help us grow in sanctification? Why do we neglect the wisdom and insight of men who are called and gifted to shepherd God's flock?

There is barely a pastor in America who is not helping someone fight against pornography. Your story won't be anything new. Be willing to go ask for help. Set aside your pride and shame, and humble yourself. Don't let the fact that pornography and masturbation are hidden sins delude you into thinking they are uncommon sins. The male struggle against sexual temptation is essentially universal. Do you think maybe your pastor will respond by saying, "I'm just shocked. You're the last person I thought would ever have this struggle." Trust me, that won't happen. Instead, I can almost guarantee he will empathize with you and be both willing and eager to help you fight and win.

While God may occasionally remove a desire to look at pornography, it is much more likely that finding freedom will be a long and difficult process. In all likelihood, you're going to need help. So cross that bridge, and make a commitment to seek help from your pastor. The local church is the ideal context for battling this kind of sin. There you will find the authority and the support to help you fight and, ultimately, to help you win.

I know some people don't have easy access to their pastors. In that case, find a trusted, mature, Christian man (make sure he meets all those qualifications!) to whom you can talk. You are not likely to have much success if you meet with a peer, someone your own age or younger. Go to a Christian man whom you love and respect and tell him what you are dealing with. It will be humbling and humiliating in all the right ways.

Let me offer a warning about accountability relationships. Although I am convinced that in many cases they can be very helpful, they also present a subtle danger. It is possible that we can come to fear an accountability partner more than we fear the Lord. Fear of God can take a back seat to fear of man as our desire to honor God is overshadowed by our desire to have only good things to report at our next accountability meeting. I'm not even talking about the temptation to lie at the meeting. I'm talking about what goes in your heart as you fight against sexual temptation. One day you're fighting for God's glory, and the next you're fighting to avoid shame before man.

We should want to grow in sanctification, not to impress others or reduce personal discomfort, but to honor God increasingly in all things. Writing of the value of mutual support within a local church community, Paul Tripp says, "The purpose of the relationship is not to *catch* the other person doing wrong, but to motivate and encourage him or her to do what is right. We minister to one another knowing that while the law is able to reveal sin, only grace can deliver us from it!" Find a person who is motivated, not to catch you in your sin, but to encourage you, pray for you, and rebuke you if necessary. In other words, find yourself a true mentor.

Purity and Your Future

It can be easy to think that the occasional look at pornography, images to fuel masturbation, will have no consequences. But if you have thought that, if you still think that, you are wrong. These are sins against God and against your present or future wife, and damaging to yourself. Every single act of sexual sin reduces your ability to be an effective leader and an effective lover.

When you sin sexually, whether before marriage or during marriage, you pile all kinds of baggage onto the back of that present or future marriage relationship. As a result, the relationship is forced to carry a weight that is unnecessarily heavy and unnecessarily complicating. Things that could have been easier become harder, sometimes permanently. Complications and temptations emerge that never had to emerge. Yes, our God is gracious and forgiving toward every repentant sinner, but there are consequences to sin that even God's forgiveness may not fully erase.

So do not mock God's grace and thumb your nose at his forbearance. Do not defraud your wife—even if you have not met her yet. Do not defraud yourself or that precious relationship. Do not defraud your children, present or future, by rendering yourself less capable of giving them a model of married life that honors God, upholds the Scriptures, and sets a godly, biblical standard.

If a young man could look ahead and see what life would be like without the baggage of sexual sin— what marriage would be like if he had taken greater advantage of the grace of God—he would cry out to God to be stronger, and God would meet that cry. Whether you are single or married, it's not too late to cry out now. It's not too late to stop adding to the baggage. It's not too late to detox. In his mercy God will begin to purify you, and he will remove some of that baggage, perhaps nearly all of it.

My encouragement to you in this is to allow all the resources of God's grace to motivate you toward moral purity. Key among these are the Bible, prayer, and a reliance on God's grace and power for the exercise of self-control. Keep in the forefront of your mind that Jesus Christ had all your sexual sin loaded upon him at the cross. He faced the just punishment for that sin and he faced the full fury of God's wrath for it; he faced the death your sin demands. By rising from the dead, he showed that he had triumphed over death. He now offers life, and he offers freedom—freedom from sin, freedom even from the desire to sin.

Some men can turn away from pornography by an act of the will. If that's you, then great: go for it. Some can do it by constructing walls of legalism and forcing themselves to live within those boundaries. This approach trades the sinful self-focus of pornography for the sinful self-reliance of legalism, so I can't encourage that approach with any enthusiasm. Many men, probably most, need outside help—a form of accountability that emphasizes encouragement and honesty, and rejects condemnation and legalism. So whether this is a battle you fight with God, or with God plus brothers in Christ, you must ultimately find freedom through the Word of God. We need to fight sin with God's truth; we need to replace the lies we want to believe with what God says is true. Perhaps some of the verses that God used in my life will help you; perhaps he will help you find others. But in any case, go to the Bible and find there both the foundation for purity and the wisdom that can help you moment-by-moment.

Some of the most tragic emails I receive through my online ministry come from women in their 40s and 50s. They relate tales of utter devastation—of husbands who got into pornography when they were young and who never cared to give it up. And here they are, all these years later, still damaging themselves and their wives and families. The choices they made as young men threaten to tear apart their families today. They never gave up their sin; they held onto it, nurtured it, acted on it for all of these years. The women, the ones God calls these men to be intoxicated with for all of their lives, live with gaping holes in their hearts, longing for their husbands to step in and fill them up.

Could this be your wife someday?

The fact is, God does not give us free passes when it comes to sin; he does not allow us to run wild for a time and just "get away with it." Sin carries consequences, whether you sin at eighteen or eighty. Turn from your sin today. Pursue freedom. Pursue Christ.

Think

1. In your heart, do you hope to have a long and sweet and normal sexual relationship with your wife? Or do you feel that you will be unfulfilled without attempting the kind of deeds you may have seen in pornography?

2. Have you ever found yourself believing that what you do morally does not really matter very much in the big picture of life? Do you believe that sins you commit today could have consequences for you and for your family many years from now?

3. Do you believe that the Bible offers not only big-picture help and guidance but also moment-by-moment help and guidance in the moment-by-moment challenges of life?

4. Do you have pastors you are able to turn to when struggling with this sin or any other? How about older men who may be willing to mentor you?

5. If you are still looking at pornography, are you willing today to go today and talk to your pastor or your father or a mentor about your problem?

6. Have any of the passages that proved helpful to me been helpful to you? Which ones and why?

7. Which Scripture verses do you intend to use as a goal, or as a measure of your desire to have a successful and God-glorifying sexual relationship with your wife? If you don't know which verses, how will you find them?

Sources Cited

Dobson, James. *Preparing for Adolescence* (Gospel Light, 1978)

Harris, Joshua. *Sex Is Not the Problem, Lust Is*, (Multnomah, 2003)

Levitt, Stephen D. & Dubner, Stephen J. *Superfreakonomics* (HarperCollins, 2009)

Lewis, C.S. *Mere Christianity* (HarperCollins, 1952)

Perkins, Bill. *When Good Men Are Tempted* (Zondervan, 1997)

Tripp, Paul David. *Broken Down House* (Shepherd Press, 2009)

Acknowledgments

Thanks to the men of Grace Fellowship Church, Toronto, for their support and assistance in preparing this book. Their honest answers to difficult questions helped me understand which issues to address.

Thanks to the readers of my blog who offered valuable feedback to the series of articles that formed the foundation for this book.

Thanks to my my wife and children for their unflagging support.

Thanks to you for reading this book. If you have questions or comments, please contact me at: tim@cruciformpress.com

Story of the Book: Sexual Detox

This is the book that helped launch an unusual little publishing company. In fact, the story of this book and the story of the formation of Cruciform Press are almost inseparable. Here, in brief, is how it happened

In August of 2009, Tim Challies began a dialogue with Kevin Meath about book editing. Before long the conversation between the two freelancers began to range into the intersection of publishing and digital technology. Soon the idea of a business was beginning to form.

In recent years the music industry had been changed—rapidly, radically, and forever—as technology redefined how people obtain and enjoy music. Something similar had begun to happen in print publishing, although a little more slowly, with technology altering how and when we read, as well as our expectations about reading. So the two men decided that, if they were to start a business, it would have to be built around the answer to a single question:

> *What would a book publishing company targeted to gospel-centered Christians look like if it began from the realities of 21st century technology?*

The idea was intriguing, but both men were too busy with other projects to pursue it further.

In November, Tim composed a series of blog posts

he called "Sexual Detox." The result of numerous long conversations with young men, this series was used by God to help many young men identify and deal with the sexual toxins in their lives due to pornography. Tim subsequently compiled the series into an ebook. He made it freely available through his blog, from where it was downloaded tens of thousands of times.

Responding to repeated requests to make the book available in a printed format, Tim turned to Kevin for help. This reignited their conversation about a company, and they soon realized they may have already begun working together on that company's first book. But the more seriously they talked about starting a business, the clearer it became that they would need some help. In March 2010, they turned to a mutual friend, Bob Bevington, a veteran of many business startups and a Christian author in his own right. Bob loved the idea, and a few weeks later the three began the real work of establishing Cruciform Press.

Sexual Detox is our first book. Targeted squarely at men—and not just young men, but men of all ages—and dealing with an issue of extraordinary scope, it is our hope that this book will help many more men understand God's call on their lives to flee youthful lusts and to pursue purity. We hope and trust also that by the grace of God we will be able to continue publishing books that are short, clear, creative, and biblical, books that draw your heart to the unending glories of the gospel of Christ, which has rich application to every area of life.

Licensed to Kill
A Field Manual for Mortifying Sin

by Brian G. Hedges

**Your soul is a war zone.
Know your enemy.
Learn to fight.**

"A faithful, smart, Word-centered guide."
– Wes Ward, *Revive Our Hearts*

"Are there things you hate that you end up doing anyway? Have you tried to stop sinning in certain areas of your life, only to face defeat over and over again? If you're ready to get serious about sin patterns in your life—ready to put sin to death instead of trying to manage it—this book outlines the only strategy that works. This is a book I will return to and regularly recommend to others."
Bob Lepine, Co-Host, *FamilyLife Today*

"Brian Hedges shows the importance of fighting the sin that so easily entangles us and robs us of our freedom, by fleeing to the finished work of Christ every day. Well done!"
Tullian Tchividjian, Coral Ridge Presbyterian Church

"Rather than aiming at simple moral reformation, *Licensed to Kill* aims at our spiritual transformation. Like any good field manual, this one focuses on the most critical information regarding our enemy, and gives practical instruction concerning the stalking and killing of sin. This is a theologically solid and helpfully illustrated book that holds out the gospel confidence of sin's ultimate demise."
Joe Thorn, pastor and author, *Note to Self: The Discipline of Preaching to Yourself*

"But God..."
The Two Words at the Heart of the
Gospel

by Casey Lute

**Just two words.
Understand their use in Scripture,
and you will never be the same.**

"Rock-solid theology packaged in an
engaging and accessible form."
– **Louis Tullo, Sight Regained blog**

"Keying off of nine occurrences of "But God" in the English Bible,
Casey Lute ably opens up Scripture in a manner that is instructive,
edifying, encouraging, and convicting. This little book would be use-
ful in family or personal reading, or as a gift to a friend. You will enjoy
Casey's style, you will have a fresh view of some critical Scripture,
and your appreciation for God's mighty grace will be deepened."
**Dan Phillips, Pyromaniacs blog, author of *The World-Tilting
Gospel* (forthcoming from Kregel)**

"A refreshingly concise, yet comprehensive biblical theology of grace
that left this reader more in awe of the grace of God."
Aaron Armstrong, BloggingTheologically.com

""Casey Lute reminds us that nothing is impossible with God, that we
must always reckon with God, and that God brings life out of death
and joy out of sorrow."
**Thomas R. Schreiner, Professor of New Testament
Interpretation, The Southern Baptist Theological Seminary**

"A mini-theology that will speak to the needs of every reader of this
small but powerful book. Read it yourself and you will be blessed.
Give it to a friend and you will be a blessing."
William Varner, Prof. of Biblical Studies, The Master's College

Smooth Stones
Bringing Down the Giant
Questions of Apologetics

by Joe Coffey

Street-level apologetics for everyday Christians.

Because faith in Jesus makes sense. And you don't need an advanced degree to understand why.

"What a thrill for me to see Joe Coffey, a graduate of our first Centurions Program class, apply the biblical worldview principles we teach at BreakPoint and the Colson Center. In this marvelous little book, Joe simply and succinctly lays out the tenets of the Christian faith within the context of the four key life and worldview questions. This is an excellent resource for Christians and non-Christians alike who are seeking the Truth."

Chuck Colson, Founder of Prison Fellowship and the Colson Center for Christian Worldview

"This book may be the best resource I've seen to answer common objections in everyday language."

Jared Totten, *Critical Thinking Blog*

"A quick read that packs a punch....I'm always on the lookout for something like this. *Smooth Stones* is a winner."

Mike del Rosario, *ApologeticsGuy.Com*

"Most books on apologetics are too long, too deep, and too complicated. This book has none of these defects. Like its title, it is like a smooth stone from David's apologetic sling directed right to the mind of an enquiring reader"

Norman L. Geisler, Distinguished Professor of Apologetics, Veritas Evangelical Seminary, Murrieta, CA

Servanthood as Worship
The Privilege of Life in a Local Church

by Nate Palmer

We [serve] because he first [served] us. – 1 John 1:19 [sort of]

What ever happened to servant-hood? Here is a biblical presentation of our calling to serve in the church, motivated by the grace that is ours in the gospel.

"In an age where the church can be likened to Cinderella - beautiful, but largely ignored and forgotten - Nate Palmer's brief book forces us to rethink both the church and our relationship to her. In an age where egocentrism ensures we sing, 'O say, can you see - what's in it for me?' on a weekly basis, Palmer forces us to say instead, 'How can I best serve the church?' Looking at the needs of others rather than one's own is possibly the most serious deficiency in the church today. Reading this book will help redress the deficiency. I heartily recommend it."
Derek W.H. Thomas, Professor of Theology
Reformed Theological Seminary (Jackson)

"Think of these pages as a handbook. It contains a sustainable, practical vision for serving in the local church that is powered by grace. Along the way, you'll get a mini theological education."
Justin Buzzard, pastor, San Francisco Bay Area, Buzzard Blog

"In our media-crazed, me-first culture, the art of the basin and the towel has been shoved off onto those who get paid to serve - certainly a call to serve in humility can't be God's will for all of us, or could it? Nate Palmer gets at the heart of our resistance.. I strongly recommend this book."
Elyse Fitzpatrick, author of Because He Loves Me

Cruciform
Living the Cross-Shaped Life

by Jimmy Davis

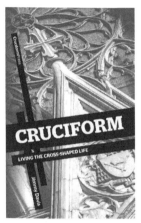

"Jimmy Davis loves the cross. This little book will open your heart up to see how the cross is the center of all of life. Well done."
— Paul Miller, Director of seeJesus. net, author of *A Praying Life*

"Jimmy Davis shows us how to cut through the fog of contemporary Christian thinking to recover the Savior's plan for our lives."
T. M. Moore, Dean, Chuck Colson's Centurions Program

"Jimmy shows from personal experience how a lack of passion and purpose, focus and fervor, compassion and conviction, is always due to distance from the now-power of the gospel. I pray that through this book you will rediscover the beauty and brilliance of the gospel in brand new ways."
Tullian Tchividjian, Coral Ridge Presbyterian Church

"*Cruciform* is a theologically grounded and redemptively freeing picture of a life spent boasting in the cross of Jesus."
Scotty Smith, Christ Community Church

"This book will be a help to everyone struggling with 'Why, God?' I believe every person planning for, and serving, in a place of Christian ministry should read this book."
Dr. Brian Richardson, Southern Baptist Theological Seminary

"This is a terrific book for those breakfast discipleship groups. It is the next one I am going to use."
Dr. William E. Brown, President, Cedarville University

CRUCIFORM EXTRA

"Comfort for the Tempted"

A Sermon by Charles Spurgeon on First
Corinthians 10:13

*Cruciform Extras are included whenever we are able
to provide helpful material, at no extra charge, that is
directly relevant to the subject matter of a book. Here
we offer in its entirety a sermon by Charles Spurgeon
on First Corinthians 10:13. This, of course, is one of the
Bible's key verses on resisting temptation of all kinds,
especially—as countless Christian men could surely
testify—sexual temptation.*

*In Spurgeon's day, public talk about sexual tempta-
tion was typically veiled in euphemisms. There's no direct
reference here to masturbation, lewd images, or crude
stories. But make no mistake, the essential issues of
temptation that men struggle with today were the same
in the 1880s. This sermon may employ a different vocabu-
lary than Sexual Detox, but it speaks the same language.*

A Sermon Delivered by Charles H. Spurgeon At the Metropolitan Tabernacle, Newington On Thursday Evening, September 27th, 1883
This sermon is based on the King James Version.

"There hath no temptation taken you but such as is common to man: but God is faithful, who will not suffer you to be tempted above that ye are able; but will with the temptation also make a way to escape, that ye may be able to bear it." — 1 Corinthians 10:13

THE CHILDREN OF GOD are all subject to temptation; some of them are tempted more than others, but I am persuaded that there is not one, except those who are too young to be conscious of evil, who will enter heaven without having endured some temptation. If anyone could have escaped, surely it would have been "the firstborn among many brethren;" but you will remember how he was led of the Spirit, straight from the waters of his baptism, into the wilderness to be tempted of the devil; and the apostle Paul informs us that he "was in all points tempted like as we are, yet without sin." Truly, the Lord Jesus might say to us who are his followers, "If I, your Master and Lord, have been tempted, you must not expect to escape temptation; for the disciple is not above his Master, nor the servant above his Lord."

The fact that we are tempted ought to humble us, for it is sad evidence that there is sin still remaining in us. I am old enough to remember the times when we used to strike with a flint upon the steel in order to get a light in the morning, and I recollect that I always left off trying to produce a spark when I found that there was no tinder in the box. I believe that the devil is no fool, and that, if there be a man who has no tinder in the box, — that is, no corruption in his nature, — depend upon it, Satan will not long continue to tempt him. He does not waste his time in such a useless exercise. The man who believes that he is perfect can never pray the Lord's prayer; he must offer one of his own making, for he will never be willing to say, "Lead us not into temptation;" but, beloved, because the devil thinks it worth his while to tempt us, we may conclude that there is something in us that is temptable, — that sin still dwells there, notwithstanding that the grace of God has renewed our hearts.

The fact that we are tempted ought also to remind us of our weakness. I referred just now to the model prayer of our Lord Jesus Christ, which contains the sentence, "Lead us not into temptation." The reason for presenting that petition must be, because we are so weak and frail. We ask that we may not be burdened, for our back is not strong; and we plead that we may not have sin put before us in any of its enticing forms, for, oftentimes, the flesh borrows strength from the world, and even from the devil, and these allied powers will be too much for us unless the omnipotence of God shall be exerted on our behalf to hold us up lest we fall.

Some children of God, whom I know of, are very greatly troubled, because they are tempted. They think they could bear trial if it were trial dissociated from sin, though I do not see how we can, as a general rule, separate trial from temptation, for every trial that comes to us has in it some kind of temptation or other, either to unbelief, or to murmuring, or to the use of wrong means to escape from the trial. We are tempted by our mercies, and we are tempted by our miseries; that is, tempted in the sense of being tried by them; but, to the child of God, the most grievous thing is that, sometimes, he is tempted to do or say things which he utterly hates. He has set before him, in a pleasant aspect, sins which are perfectly abhorrent to him; he cannot bear the very name of them. Yet Satan comes, and holds before the child of God the unclean meats which he will never touch; and I have known the devil to tempt the people of God by injecting into their mind blasphemous thoughts, hurling them into their ear as with a hurricane. Ay, even when you are in prayer, it may happen to you that thoughts the very opposite of devotional will come flocking into your brain. A little noise in the street will draw you off from communion with God; and, almost before you are aware of it, your thoughts, like wild horses, will have gone galloping over hill and dale, and you hardly know how you shall ever catch them again. Now, such temptations as these are dreadfully painful to a child of God. He cannot bear the poisoned breath of sin; and when he finds that sin stands knocking at his door, shouting under his window, pestering him day and night, as it has occurred with some, —I hope not with many,—then he is sorely beset, and he is grievously troubled.

It may help such a person if I remind him that there is no sin in being tempted. The sin is that of the tempter, not of the tempted. If you resist the temptation, there is something praiseworthy about your action. There is nothing praiseworthy about the temptation; that is evil, and only evil; but you did not tempt yourself, and he that tempted yon must bear the blame of the temptation. You are evidently not blameworthy for thoughts that grieve you; they may prove that there is sin still remaining in you, but there is no sin in your being tempted. The sin is in your yielding to the temptation, and blessed shall you be if you can stand out against it. If you can overcome it, if your spirit does not yield to it, you shall even be blessed through it. "Blessed is the man that endureth temptation." There is a blessedness even in the temptation, and though for the present it seemeth not to be joyous, but grievous, nevertheless, afterward, it yieldeth blessed fruit to those who are exercised thereby.

Moreover, there are worse things in this world than being tempted with painful temptations. It is much worse to be tempted with a pleasant temptation,—to be gently sucked down into the destroyer's mouth,—to be carried along the smooth current, afterwards to be hurled over the cataract. This is dreadful; but to fight against temptation,—this is good. I say again that there are many worse things than to be tried with a temptation that arouses all the indignation of your spirit. An old divine used to say that he was more afraid of a sleeping devil than he was of a roaring one, and there is much truth in that observation; for, when you are left quite alone, and no temptation assails you, you are apt to get carnally secure, and boastfully to say, "I shall never be moved." I think no man is in such imminent danger as the man who thinks that there is no danger likely to befall him, so that anything that keeps us on the watch-tower, even though it be in itself evil, is, so far, overruled for good. The most dangerous part of the road to heaven is not the Valley of the Shadow of Death; we do not find that Christian went to sleep there when the hobgoblins were all about him, and when he found it hard to feel the path, and keep to it; but when he and Hopeful came to the Enchanted Ground, "whose air naturally tended to make one drowsy," then were the pilgrims in great peril until Christian reminded his fellow-traveler that they were warned by the shepherds not to sleep when they came to that treacherous part of the way. I think, then, that to be tempted with painful temptations, those that goad the spirit almost to madness,—bad as that trial is,—grievous as it is to be borne,—may be, spiritually, not the worst thing that can possibly happen to us. Of all evils that beset you, always choose that which is less than another; and as this is less than something else might be, do not be utterly driven to despair if it falls to your lot to be tempted as many before you have been.

This will suffice by way of preface to a little talk about temptation, with a view of comforting any who are sorely tempted of Satan. I know that I am speaking to many such, and I would repeat to them the words of my text: "There hath no temptation taken you but such as is common to man: but God is faithful, who will not suffer you to be tempted above that ye are able; but will with the temptation also made a way to escape, that ye may be able to bear it." Remember, dear tried friend, that you must not sit down in despair, and say, "I am greatly tempted now, and I am afraid that I shall be tempted worse and worse, until my feet shall slide, and I shall fall and utterly perish." Do not say as David did when he had been hunted like a partridge upon the mountains, "I shall now perish one day by the hand of Saul;" but believe that the Lord, who permits you to be tempted, will deliver you in his own good time.

I. Here is your first comfort. THERE HAS BEEN A LIMIT IN ALL YOUR FORMER TRIALS: "There hath no temptation taken you but such as is common to man."

Temptation has sometimes laid hold of you, like a garroter takes a man by the throat, on a sudden. It has seized you,— perhaps that is as correct a word as I can use,—temptation has seized you, unawares, pinioned you, and seemed to grip you fast; and yet, up till now, the temptations you have had to endure, have only been such as are common to man.

First, they are such as have been endured by your fellow-Christians. I know that you are tempted to think that you are a lone traveler on a road that nobody has ever traversed before you; but if you carefully examine the track, you can discover the footprints of some of the best of God's servants who have passed along that wearisome way. It is a very dark lane, you say,—one that might truly be called, "Cut-throat Lane." Ah! but you will find that apostles have been along that way, confessors have been that way, martyrs have been that way, and the best of God's saints have been tempted just as you now are. "Oh, but!" says one, "I am tempted, as you said a little while ago, with blasphemous and horrible thoughts." So was Master John Bunyan; read his Grace Abounding to the Chief of Sinners, and see what he had to pass through. Many others have had a similar experience, and among them are some of us who are alive to tell you that we know all about this special form of temptation, yet the Lord delivered us out of it. "Oh, but!" says another tried soul, "I have been even tempted to self-destruction." That also has not been an unusual temptation even to God's dearest saints; and, though he has preserved them, and kept them alive, yet they have often felt like Job when he said, "My soul chooseth strangling, and death rather than my life." "Ah!" cries another, "I am tempted to the very worst sins, the foulest sins, I should not dare even to mention to you the abominations Satan tempts me to commit." You need not tell me; and I trust that you will be kept from them by the almighty power of God's Holy Spirit; but I can assure you that even the saints in heaven, if they could speak to you at this moment, would tell you that some of them were hard beset—even some of the bravest of them who walked nearest to God were hard beset by temptations which they would not have told to their fellow-men, so troubled were they by them. Perhaps yet another friend says, "I have been actually tempted to self-righteousness, which is as great a temptation as can befall a man whose whole confidence is in Christ." Well, so was Master John Knox, that grand preacher of justification by faith. When he lay dying, he was tempted to glory in his own bravery for Christ, but he fought against that evil thought, and overcame it, and so may you.

You think that, when a man is very patient, he is not tempted to impatience. Brother, the Spirit of God says, by the pen of the apostle James, "Ye have heard of the patience of Job." I suggest to you this question,—Have you not heard of the impatience of Job? You have heard, no doubt, of the strong faith of Peter; have you never heard of Peter's unbelief? God's people usually fail in the very point for which they are most famous; and the man who has the greatest renown for any work of the Spirit of God in him, so far as the Bible biographies are concerned, has usually been the man who has made a failure just at the place where he thought he was strongest. "I have been reading the life of a good man," say you, "and I am not like him." Shall I tell you why? Because the whole of his life was not written; but when the Holy Ghost writes a man's life, he gives it all. When biographers write the lives of good men, of course they do not put down their inward struggles and fears, unless the subject happens to be a man like Martin Luther, whose life seemed to be all an inward struggle, and who, while he was brave without, was often a trembler within. When they write my life, they will tell you that I had strong faith; but they will not tell you all about the other side of it. And then you will, perhaps, get thinking, "Oh, I cannot reach even to such a height as Mr. Spurgeon attained!" That all comes of your not knowing the inside of us, for if you knew the inside and the outside of the man who walks nearest to God, — if he is a sincere, truehearted man, he will tell you that the temptations you have to endure are just such temptations as he has had, and as he expects to have again and again, and that, as the apostle says, "there hath no temptation taken you but such as is common to man."

Then, again, no temptation has assailed you but such as fit for men to be tried with while they are in this state of trial. This is not the time for the final victory, brother; this is the hour of battle, and the weapons that are used against us are only such as have been employed against the armies of the faithful in all ages. You and I never were tempted as were the angels who kept their first estate and overcame the temptation. I cannot tell you how the prince of darkness was tempted, or how he went about tempting his fellow-servants from their loyalty to the great King; but of this I am sure, you were never tried with a temptation suitable to an angel. Your temptation has only been such as is suitable to a man, and such as other men like yourself have overcome. Others have fought valiantly against similar temptations to yours, and you must do the same, yea, and you shall do the same by the power of God's Spirit resting upon you. It is said, in the affairs of common life, that what man has done man can do, and that is true with regard to the spiritual life. Temptations that have been grappled with by other men, can be grappled with by you if you seek the same source of strength, and seek it in the same name as they did. The strength to overcome temptation comes from God alone, and the conquering name is the name of Jesus Christ; therefore, go forward in that strength and in that name against all your temptations. Up and at them, for they have been routed long before, and you shall rout them again. Tremble not to go from fight to fight and from victory to victory, even as did the others who have gone before you, and who have now entered into their rest.

> Once they were mourning here below,
> And wet their couch with tears;
> They wrestled hard, as we do now,
> With sins, and doubts, and fears.

If you ask them whence their victory came, they ascribe it to the resources which are as open to you as they were to them,— even to the mighty working of God the Holy Spirit and the blood and righteousness of the Lord Jesus Christ. There has no temptation happened to you but such as human beings can grapple with and overcome by the help of God.

Again, there has no temptation hitherto happened to you but such as is common to man in this sense,—that Christ has endured it. That great Head of manhood, that representative Man, has suffered from the very temptation which is now pestering you. "In all their affliction"—that is, the affliction of his people in the wilderness, which is just the same as yours if you are in the wilderness,—"in all their affliction he was afflicted, and the angel of his presence saved them." He was compassed with infirmity, "a man of sorrows and acquainted with grief." To repeat the text I have already quoted, and which is so suitable here, he "was in all points tempted like as we are." "In all things it behoved him to be made like unto his brethren, that he might be a merciful and faithful high priest in things pertaining to God, to make reconciliation for the sins of the people. For in that he himself hath suffered being tempted, he is able to succor them that are tempted." He knows all about the case of each one of us, and he knows how to deal with it, and how to bear us up and bear us through.

So you see, dear friends, there hath no temptation happened to you but such as is common to man in the sense of having been endured by men like yourselves, having been overcome by men such as you are, and having been endured and vanquished by your blessed Representative, our Lord and Savior Jesus Christ.

Come, then, beloved, let all mystery with regard to your temptations be banished. Mystery puts an edge upon the sword of trial; perhaps the hand that wrote upon the wall would not have frightened Belshazzar if he could have seen the body to which that hand belonged. There is no mystery about your trouble, after all. Though you did write it down as being bigger than any that ever happened to a human being before, that is not the truth; you are not an emperor in the realm of misery. You cannot truly say, "I am the man that hath seen affliction above all others," for your Lord endured far more than you have ever done, and many of his saints, who passed from the stake to the crown, must have suffered much more than you have been called to undergo thus far.

II. Now let us turn to the second comfort revealed in our text; that is, THE FAITHFULNESS OF GOD: "There hath no temptation taken you but such as is common to man: but God is faithful."

Oh, what a blessed word is this, "God is faithful"! Therefore, He is true to his promise. Even Balaam said, "God is not a man, that he should lie; neither the son of man, that he should repent: hath he said, and shall he not do it? or hath he spoken, and shall he not make it good?" One of God's promises is, "I will never leave thee, nor forsake thee;" "God is faithful," so he will fulfill that promise. Here is one of the promises of Christ, and Christ is God: "My sheep hear my voice, and I know them, and they follow me: and I give unto them eternal life; and they shall never perish, neither shall any man pluck them out of my hand." "God is faithful," so that promise shall be fulfilled. You have often heard this promise, "As thy days, so shall thy strength be." Do you believe it, or will you make God a liar? If you do believe it, then banish from your mind all dark forebodings with this blessed little sentence, "God is faithful."

Notice, next, that not only is God faithful, but He is master of the situation, so that he can keep his promise. Note what the text says: "Who will not suffer you to be tempted above that ye are able to bear." Then you could not have been tempted if God had not suffered it to happen to you. God is far mightier than Satan. The devil could not touch Job except by divine permission, neither can he try and tempt you except as God allows him; he must have a permit from the King of kings before he can tempt a single saint. Why, Satan is not allowed to keep the key of his own house, for the keys of death and of hell hang at the girdle of Christ; and without God's permission, the dog of hell cannot even open his mouth to bark at a child of God, much less can he come and worry any of the sheep whom the Lord has called by his grace into his fold. So, then, beloved, you have great cause for comfort from the fact that the temptation that tries you is still under the control of the faithful Creator, "who will not suffer you to be tempted above that ye are able."

That is a second reason for comfort; roll it under your tongue as a sweet morsel.

III. The third comfort lies in THE RESTRAINT WHICH GOD PUTS UPON TEMPTATION. He "will not suffer you to be tempted above that ye are able." The tide of trial shall rise to high-water mark, and then God shall say, "Hitherto shalt thou come, but no further: and here shall thy proud waves be stayed."

He "will not suffer you to be tempted above that ye are able." That may apply, sometimes, to the period when the temptation comes. I have carefully watched how God times the trials of his people. If such-and-such a trial had come to one of his children when he was young, I believe he could not have borne it; or if he had lost some dear friend while he was himself sick, the double trouble would have crushed him. But God sends our trials at the right time; and if he puts an extra burden on in one way, he takes something off in another. "He stayeth his rough wind in the day of the East wind." It is a very simple thing to say, but it is true; if the wind blows from the North, it does not at the same time blow from the South; and if one set of troubles comes to a Christian man, another set of troubles generally departs from him. John Bradford, the famous martyr, was often subject to rheumatism and depres-

sion of spirit, in which I can greatly sympathize with him; but when
he was laid by the heels in a foul damp dungeon, and knew that
he would never come out except to die, he wrote, "It is a singular
thing that, ever since I have been in this prison, and have had
other trials to bear, I have had no touch of my rheumatism or my
depression of spirit." Was not that a very blessed thing? And you
will usually find that it is so; you shall not be tempted above what
you are able to bear, because God will permit the trial to come at a
time when you are best able to stand up under it.

There is also great kindness on God's part in the continuance
of a trial. If some of our trials lasted much longer, they would be
too heavy for us to bear. Concerning the destruction of Jerusalem,
our Lord said, "Except those days should be shortened, there
should no flesh be saved: but for the elect's sake those days shall
be shortened." And I have no doubt that, oftentimes, God makes
quick work of his children's trials because, if they were continued
longer, they would have not a good but an evil effect upon us. If a
child must be whipped, let not the punishment last as if he were a
criminal who must be sentenced for a long period; let him have his
chastisement, and have done with it. So is it often in the discipline
of God's house; yet there are other trials which are protracted year
after year because trial is an ingredient in their efficacy, and they
might not be blessed to us if they were shortened. In every case,
there is an infinite wisdom which makes our troubles to be just as
long as they are, and no longer.

So there is in the number of the trials. Blessed be God, —

If he ordains the number ten,
They ne'er can be eleven.

If he intends his servants to pass through the fire, and not
through the water, Satan himself cannot make them go through
the water. God counts the drops of bitter tonic that he administers
to his ailing saints, and not a drop more shall they possibly have
than he measures out to them. So, dear tried children of God, you
shall not be tempted above what ye are able so far as the number
of your temptations and trials is concerned.

It is the same, also, in the stress with which the temptation comes. Have you never seen a great tree in the full blast of a tremendous tempest? It sways to and fro, and seems scarcely able to recover itself from the powerful blows of the storm; yet the roots hold it. But now comes another tornado; and it seems as if the tree must be torn up out of the earth; but the strain ceases just in time for the old oak to rock back into its place again; yet, if there were a pound or two more force in that tremendous blast, the tree would be laid prone upon the grass; but God, in his people's case at any rate, just stops at the right point. You may be tried till you have not an ounce of strength left. Sometimes, the Lord tests his people till it seems as if one more breath from him would assuredly cause them to sink. Then it is that he puts under them the everlasting arms, and no further trial is laid upon them. This is a blessed thing, for all of you have troubles of one sort or another, and you who are the people of God may take this text, and, rely implicitly upon it: "God is faithful, who will not suffer you to be tempted above that ye are able." As for you who are not his people, I am very sorry for you. I am holding up these precious things, but they are not for you. God's Word declares, "Many sorrows shall be to the wicked." If you have no God to flee to, what will you do when the storms beat upon your barque? To whom or whither can you flee? As for the Christian, he can sing, —

Jesu, lover of my soul,
Let me to thy bosom fly,
While the nearer waters roll,
While the tempest still is high!
Hide me, O my Savior, hide,
Till the storm of life be past
Safe into the haven guide;
Oh receive my soul at last!

But, poor dear souls who love not Christ, where can you find comfort in your seasons of sorrow and trial? You who have lost wife and children, — you who are pinched with poverty, — you who are racked with sickness, and yet have no Savior, what can you do? Poor houseless people in a snow-storm, — what can they do without even a bush to shelter them? That is just your state, and

I grieve for you, and plead with you not to remain in such a pitiful condition even a moment longer.

> Come, guilty souls, and flee away
> Like doves to Jesu's wounds;
> This is the welcome gospel-day,
> Wherein free grace abounds.

Oh, that your sense of need might drive you to accept Christ as your Savior this very hour! As for his believing people, there is this solid comfort for them, they shall never be tempted above what they are able.

IV. The next comfort we gather from our text relates to THE PROVISION WHICH THE LORD MAKES FOR THE TEMPTED: "God is faithful, who . . . will with the temptation also make a way to escape."

The Greek has it, "who will with the temptation also make the way to escape;" for there is a proper way to escape from a temptation. There are twenty improper ways; and woe to the man who makes use of any one of them; but there is only one proper way out of a trial, and that is the straight way, the way that God has made for his people to travel. God has made through all trials the way by which his servants may rightly come out of them. When the brave young Jews were tried by Nebuchadnezzar, there was one way by which they might have kept out of the burning fiery furnace. They had only to bow their knees before the great image when the flute, harp, sackbut, and psaltery sounded; that way of escape would never have answered, for it was not the right one. The way for them was to be thrown down into the furnace, and there to have the Son of God walking with them in the midst of the fire that could not hurt them. In like manner, whenever you are exposed to any trial, mind that you do not try to escape from it in any wrong way.

Notice specially that the right way is always of God's making; therefore, any of you who are now exposed to temptation or trial have not to make your own way of escape out of it. God, and God alone, has to make it for you, so do not attempt to make it for yourselves. I knew a man who was in trouble because he was short of money; and the way he made for himself was to use somebody else's money, with which he had been entrusted. That was not God's way of escape for him, so he only plunged himself into a worse trial than he was in before. I have known a man of business in great trouble, and things were going wrong with him, so he speculated, and gambled, and ruined, both his business and his personal character. That was not God's way for him to escape from his troubles. Sometimes, the best thing a man in trouble can do, is to do nothing at all, but to leave all in the hands of God. "Stand still, and see the salvation of the Lord." When the Israelites came out of Egypt, God led them in a way at which men might well have cavilled; there was nothing before them but the sea, and behind them came Pharaoh in all his rage, crying, "I will pursue, I will overtake, I will divide the spoil; my lust shall be satisfied upon them; I will draw my sword, my hand shall destroy them." Now, then, what was God's way of escape for them? Right through the Red Sea, and on the other side they sang, when the Egyptians were drowned, "Sing ye to the Lord, for he hath triumphed gloriously; the horse and his rider hath he thrown into the sea." It would have been a great pity if they had tried to escape by any way of their own, or had attempted to turn round, and fight Pharaoh; that would not have done at all, but the Lord made for his people the very best way of escape that could possibly have been devised.

Notice, also, that the Lord makes the way of escape "with the temptation." He suffered the trial to come, and at the same time he made the way of escape from it. God has planned it all, my brother, how you, his champion, shall go forth, and fight valiantly in his strength; and how he will be your shield and your exceeding great reward. He will lead you into the dangerous fire; but then he can see the way out of it as well as the way into it, and he will take you safely through. Did not the psalmist sing, "To him which led his people through the wilderness: for his mercy endureth for ever"? He not only led them into the wilderness, but he led them through it, blessed be his holy name! And if he has brought you into the wilderness of trouble and affliction, he made the way out of it at the same time that he made the trouble. "Trust in the Lord, and do good; so shalt thou dwell in the land, and verily thou shalt be fed. Delight thyself also in the Lord; and he shall give thee the desires of thine heart. Commit thy way unto the Lord; trust also in him; and he shall bring it to pass. And he shall bring forth thy righteousness as the light, and thy judgment as the noonday. Rest in the Lord, and wait patiently for him: fret not thyself because of him who prospereth in his way, because of the man who bringeth wicked devices to pass." "Seek ye first the kingdom of God and his righteousness," and all else that you need shall be added unto you. Keep clear of the sin of the temptation, and you need not fear the sorrow of the temptation. If the trials do not drive you to your own devices, but drive you to your knees, they will, after all, be blessings to you.

That is the fourth comfort, that God has made the way of escape for his people out of their trials. "Well, then," says someone, "I shall escape from this trial." Wait a moment, my friend, and listen to the closing words of the text, with which I will conclude my discourse.

V. This is the last point of comfort, THE SUPPORT WHICH GOD SUPPLIES IN THE TRIAL: "that ye may be able to bear it."

God's way of escape from trial is not for his people to avoid it, so as not to pass through it, but such an escape as leads them through the trouble, and out at the other end; not an escape from the Red Sea, but an escape through the Red Sea frown a still greater trial. If you, beloved, are exposed to trial or temptation, you are to be made able to bear it. Now, pray, before you leave this building, that this last word, upon which I have not time to enlarge, may be fulfilled in your experience: "that ye may be able to bear it."

Suppose you are to be poor. Well, if God has so appointed it, you will be poor; therefore, pray that you may be able to bear it. With honest industry and stern integrity struggle to attain to a better position; but, if all your efforts fail, then say to the Lord, "Nevertheless, not as I will, but as thou wilt." Perhaps your dear child is dying, or your wife is sickening; you dread the thought of losing them, and you would willingly give your life, if you could, for them. Well, do all you can for their recovery, for life is precious, and any money spent to save it will be well spent; but, if health is not to be granted to them, pray that you may be able to bear even that heavy trial. It is wonderful how God does help his people to bear troubles which they thought would crush them. I have seen poor feeble women, that I thought would die under their bereavement, become brave and strong; and men, who were faint-hearted in the prospect of trouble, have nevertheless blessed the Lord for it when the blow has actually fallen; and you may do the same.

Suppose you are to be sick. Well, that is a sore trial, and I know that, personally, I would do anything I could to escape from the affliction that often besets me; but if it must not be, then I must change my note, and pray that I may be able to bear it. I had a letter from a man of God, this morning, which sustained me very much. He says, "My dear brother, I was sorry to hear that you were again in pain, and depressed in spirit, and so forth; but, as I remembered how God had blessed you in so many ways, I thought to myself, 'Perhaps Mr. Spurgeon would not have kept to preaching the doctrines of grace, and would not have been so able to comfort God's poor people, if he did not get these smart touches sometimes.' So," he said, "I congratulate you upon these trials;" and I accepted the congratulation. Will not you do the same, my afflicted brother or sister? Pray, "Lord, if it be possible, let this cup pass from me;" but, if it must not, then here comes that other form of comfort, "that ye may be able to bear it."

And remember, dear friends, while I tell you to make this passage into a prayer, it is really a promise; and there is no prayer like a promise that is turned, as it were, roundabout, and cut prayerwise. God himself has said, by his inspired apostle, that he "will not suffer you to be tempted above that ye are able; but will with the temptation also make a way to escape, that ye may be able to bear it." Up with the banners, then! Forward, whatever obstructs the way! Let us sing, with good old John Ryland, —

Through floods and flames, if Jesus lead,
I'll follow where he goes;
'Hinder me not,' shall be my cry,
Though earth and hell oppose.

The immortal life within us can never be destroyed; the divine nature, which God the Holy Ghost has implanted, shall never be trodden under foot. "Rejoice not against me, O mine enemy; when I fall, I shall arise; when I sit in darkness, the Lord shall be a light unto me."

But, oh, sorry, sorry, sorry, sorry am I, from the bottom of my soul, for you who know not the Lord, for this comfort is not for you! Seek him, I pray you; seek him as your Savior. Look to him, and trust in him; and then all the blessings of the everlasting covenant shall be yours, for the Father has given him to be a Leader and Commander unto the people, and they that look to him, and follow him, shall live forever and ever. God bless you, for Christ's sake! Amen.

CruciformPress

Website
CruciformPress.com

Newsletter
http://bit.ly/CruciformNL

Sampler
http://bit.ly/samplr

Facebook
http://on.fb.me/Cruciform

Twitter
@CruciformPress

Ebook Downloads $5.45
http://bit.ly/CPebks